THE COMPLETE GAME SHOOT

THE COMPLETE
GAME SHOOT

John Humphreys

David & Charles

BY THE SAME AUTHOR

Living Off the Land
Hides, Calls and Decoys
The Sportsman Head to Toe
Modern Pigeon Shooting
Stanley Duncan, Wildfowler
The Shooting Handbook (Ed)
The Do-It-Yourself Gameshoot
Learning to Shoot
The Woods Belong to Me (Ed)
Hunter's Fen
Shooting Pigeons
The Country Sportsman's Record Book & Journal
The Complete Gundog
Poachers' Tales
Days and Nights on Hunter's Fen
The Complete Rough Shoot

Illustrations by John Paley

A DAVID & CHARLES BOOK

Copyright © John Humphreys 1992

First published 1992

John Humphreys has asserted his right to be identified
as author of this work in accordance with the
Copyright, Designs and Patents Act 1988.

A catalogue record for this book is available from the
British Library.

ISBN 0 7153 9916 0

Typeset by ABM Typographics Ltd, Hull
and printed in Great Britain
by Redwood Press Ltd,
for David & Charles
Brunel House   Newton Abbot   Devon

Contents

Grouse Shooting, 1924.
The best cartridges to
use are————

————manufactured by

ELEY & KYNOCH

OBTAINABLE FROM ALL GUNMAKERS AND DEALERS

Introduction

The shooting of game, walked-up and driven—it matters not—has never been more popular nor more easily available. The days when the covertside and grouse butt were the privileged and exclusive terrain of the rich, famous and nobly born have long gone, and nowadays those with no ground of their own may buy days of any quality on almost any estate of their choice, from lofty grouse moor and Suffolk partridge manor to Norfolk pheasant covert.

This wonderful, traditional British field sport, with its roots deep in the eighteenth-century estates of East Anglia, Scotland and the West Country, has evolved and changed, retaining the best of the old and embracing some brave new ideas. Little did the Victorian shooting stars realise that the woods they planted for their teeming pheasants would one day be the emblem of the very countryside the latter-day conservationists wished to save: the moorland owner of 1905 might not have expected that the wild acres he saved for his red grouse would one day become one of the most rare, delicate and valuable habitats in the world.

The skills, ritual and the pure magic of the shooting day remain. The birds are fewer in number but of better quality than when Lord Ripon shot his hundreds of thousands—but more important, the shooting man, his keeper and his landlord are the custodians of the countryside and its wild inhabitants: now that the financial, political, practical pressures are at their greatest their services are needed as never before.

John Humphreys, Bottisham 1992

1
The Golden Age

Prior to the 1860s shooting men had walked up their birds, taking pheasant and more often grey partridge as they rose and flew off in front of them. The modern shotgun is still bored for such shooting, the open barrel firing first when the bird is closest, and the second, more tightly choked barrel being saved for the same bird or another when at greater range. The fact that much modern game shooting is driven seems to have passed by the barrel-makers. The early part of that century had seen shooting as a sport for the lower orders, the gentry preferring to take to the hunting field. A revolution was to occur which changed all that, and created a shooting class of sportsman which for a short generation included the highest and noblest in the land.

The reasons were several and coincidental. The muzzle-loader involved an infinitely slow process of reloading, requiring the whole field to stop and stand still whilst the palaver of powder flask, wadding, shot belt, more wadding and cap on the nipple was carefully undertaken; this made the shooting field a leisurely place. The Great Exhibition of 1855 had on display the first breech-loading sporting gun made in France by Lefeauchaux. This led to the pinfire and quickly to the centre-fire, hinged-action, breech-loading shotgun, a design which has remained basically unchanged in all but detail until the present day. The great London gunmakers and many in the provinces, especially Birmingham, were foremost in its development, and there was a period of frenzied trial and error so that patent action, ejecting system, self-opening breech and locking mechanism came and went until the ultimate was reached.

In the early days, the double-hammer gun was standard in the new-look shooting field peopled by those who had discovered the greater challenge of shooting a bird flying fast towards them, rather than one blundering up and flying away from under their feet. The great shots of the Golden Age loved their hammer guns, and some of them continued using them long after the prettier and quicker hammerless gun was in almost universal use. King George V was a distinguished example.

The new guns and the evolution of new gunpowders, more efficient and safer than the old black powder, placed a new complexion on shooting and opened up unanticipated possibilities. Lord Ripon, one of the greatest game shots ever, wrote to Purdeys about the new Schultz powder, first of the so-called 'smokeless' types: 'I find I shoot at least 30% quicker with it than with black. . . . My bag might interest you: Aug 12th . . . 650 grouse; Aug 14th . . . 500 grouse. Total 2 days 1,150. Please send me 2,000 of the same cartridges to be here by 24th August.' The bags he mentions were made to his own gun.

Guns and cartridges had also improved dramatically and were now capable of inflicting slaughter much greater than the possibilities of the walked-up day could ever present. A bonus to the sport at this time was the interest taken in it by the Prince of Wales, later King Edward VII. His figure was not suited to the hunting field and shooting seemed to offer him the company, sumptuous hospitality and lifestyle which he sought. What royalty did today, the rest of the fashionable world did tomorrow, with the result that driven shooting enjoyed a sudden boom in popularity. Income tax at 5d in the £1 meant that huge fortunes were available to develop the new shooting estates. Some of these fanatics—for example Lord Walsingham and Duleep Singh—were bankrupted by the effort of producing colossal bags of pheasants and entertaining at a Lucullan rate when house parties came for the sport.

Armies of gamekeepers were employed and rearing programmes of immense proportions were embarked upon. By 1900 the royal estate at Sandringham was rearing 12,000 pheasants in addition to the profusion of wild game already there—for this was the era of the grey partridge, when those birds were as common as sparrows and every weedy field held a few covies. However, even this programme was to look modest compared with some of what was to follow. Keepers learned new skills of game preservation, of rearing in huge numbers and preparing food for a host of hungry birds, of making shelter and release pens, and killing every real and imagined enemy of game which dared show beak or paw on the wrong side of the boundary. The Euston system produced successful partridge nests, the experiments at Elveden seemed unending, and firms such as Gilbertson and Page evolved at that time simply to meet the needs of the great new army of gamekeepers and rearers. A revolution was about to happen. As someone, somewhere, felicitously remarked, we had in the shooting field the fire power of Vimy Ridge but with a better lunch.

Another factor to hasten the new era was the development of the railways. Access to the more remote estates was now possible without a tiresome carriage journey of many days and inconvenient overnight stays. Now the aristocracy could travel quickly and in the comfort of their own railway carriages, with their customary retinue of servants without which they found it impossible to move a step. A typical caravanserai which carried Sir John Anson and his shooting party to Scotland with the Duke of Sutherland had sixteen carriages, luxuriously built even down to the staff quarters, with plenty of room for luggage, dogs and copious cartridges. The train happened to be derailed at 50 mph while passing through Wigan, with a few fatalities among the lower orders; but eventually the expedition carried on successfully.

The Prince of Wales was no exception, and when he bought the Sandringham estate—which remains a bright jewel in the royal sporting crown—he had Wolferton station built as close as possible to the house. The royal train which did the shooting run for many years is still preserved. More and more hitherto inaccessible places became easy to reach, with the added advantage that in reverse, house guests could return quite easily to London in the event of some national or commercial crisis, so they no longer felt cut off.

The development of the great driven bird shoots was made possible due to the emergence of the safe and efficient centre fire sporting gun, the rise of the railways, and the impetus of royal patronage.

The size of the bag became the all-important factor of a shooting day, and not necessarily the quality of the birds. There were those such as Lord Walsingham and Lord Ripon who did not care for the social aspect of the shooting house party but genuinely enjoyed their shooting, but others vied one with another to see who could down the greatest number. It was rumoured that as well as huge rearing programmes, some estates imported birds in crates the night before a big day, the further to swell the bag.

One of the most vaunted feats of bag-filling was that by Lord Walsingham: nettled by the rumour that the King would not visit his moor because he believed there to be few grouse on it, his lordship took wagers that he would kill 1,000 birds to his own gun in a day. What followed has entered the lore and legend of game shooting, although no-one today would care to emulate it, even if the opportunity arose. On his Blubberhouse moor in Yorkshire, his Lordship killed 1,070 grouse, which had been driven back and forth over his head by two teams of beaters. The hourglass shape of the moor favoured this feat, although many birds were, it was said, picked up too exhausted to fly again. He also shot as he made his way home and killed another six or seven brace, included in the grand total.

As for marksmanship and judgement, let there be no mistake that the best were outstanding. Take the occasion when Lords Walsingham and Ripon were shooting in Yorkshire when a covey of eight partridges flew between them. Each gun supported by a loader killed two successive rights and lefts, a feat not only of superb marksmanship but of judgement too, for not one bird was shared, each gun knowing instinctively which were his and which his neighbour's.

The great estates—including Warter Priory, Holkham, Sandringham, Elveden and Six Mile Bottom—are still names with which to conjure, although today moderation as well as quality are more acceptable. In 1913,

In the Golden Age of shooting a specially made butt would be occupied by the
Gun, one or two loaders and sometimes a lady companion. A boy to carry the
cartridges would be on hand in those days of cheap labour

3,937 pheasants were killed at Hall Barn in Buckinghamshire in a day; at
Holkham in Norfolk in 1905, 1,671 partridges were shot; while as for grouse,
there were many days when just short of the 3,000-head mark were
accounted for. Rabbits in the pre-myxomatosis days swarmed and were
popular—if dangerous—sport. On 7 Oct 1898 at Blenheim 6,943 were shot;
and three years earlier in Wales, 5,086 were accounted for.

As for individual feats, as well as the aforementioned grouse shoot by
Lord Walsingham, there was Duleep Singh with his 780 partridges at
Eleveden to his own gun in a day. Lord de Grey shot 240 partridges in a
single drive, and various of the big shots killed slightly fewer than 500
grouse in a day, usually over pointers. The shooting world was one of
plentiful birds, a rich environment unspoiled by sprays and modern
farming, peopled largely by those with the time and money to shoot, and
last but not least, an uncritical public.

The greatest feat of all was the performance by the second Marquis of
Ripon between the years 1867 and 1923, who shot to his own gun the
following: 124,193 partridges, 241,224 pheasants, a similar number of
grouse, and innumerable head of all shootable species including tiger and
even a brace of rhinoceros. His grand total was 556,813 head of game. 1890
was his best year, with a personal bag of 18,500.

These excesses had within them the seeds of their own destruction. There
was a limit, surely, and it was being reached: the flow of money to support
such an impossibly lavish shooting lifestyle was vast, but it was not
bottomless. Also, slaughter in the trenches on the Western Front had
provoked a pause for thought concerning the mounds of the slain in the
shooting field; besides, the keepers and shoot helpers had gone to the

trenches along with many of their masters, never to return. Sir Ralph Payne Gallwey was one of the great shots, and his own son was amongst those who went overseas, not to be seen again.

There was a taking stock and a rethinking of the whole business. George V and George VI were great shots also and occasionally shot big bags; however, George V was very silent after a 4,000-odd pheasant day and was heard to remark quietly, 'I think we may have overdone it today'—surely a sign of a crack in the wall. Walsingham would never have divested himself of such a sentiment.

Lord Ripon on How to Shoot

To be a first-rate shot necessitates the combination of two distinctly opposite conditions: a highly strung nervous temperament which keeps you ever on the alert, a cool head which enables you in moments of excitement to fire without recklessness or undue haste. This combination is naturally rare. That 'practice makes perfect' is in the case of shooting only true to a certain extent, for a man must be born with a certain inherent aptitude to become a really first-rate shot.

The great thing for a beginner is not to lose heart, and to those who realise that proficiency in any art means hard work and perseverance, I offer the following suggestions, which are the result of long experience.

One of the first points to be considered is that of standing so as to be prepared for every variety of shot. If the bird is flying to your right, your left leg should be forward: if to the left, your right leg. This is most important, and I have improved the shooting of several of my friends quite twenty-five per cent by showing them how to stand.

Quickness in letting off the second or even the third gun is no doubt to a great extent a matter of practice. Never look at your gun or your loader, for while your hands should be ever ready to receive the gun from him, your eyes should be concentrated on the birds. A quick shooter will fire his two guns and four barrels almost as if they were on one stock.

It is also most necessary to acquire and cultivate judgment of distance. Some men never know if a bird is forty or sixty yards off, others are apt to consider the object out of shot when it is not more than fifty yards from the muzzle of the gun.

When birds are coming in great numbers, always select one to shoot at, and do not vacillate, whatever happens. Many men who are good shots at single birds miss when they are obliged to choose one out of a lot to fire at, simply from inability to make up their minds in time. It is a question of quick selection and judgment, the latter quality being also all-important in the case of the *angle* at which the bird should be shot. Nearly every shooter has his favourite angle— that is to say, given plenty of time, he shoots at his bird when it reaches the angle he prefers: but this tendency can be carried too far and should not be encouraged, for a man often gets into the habit of waiting for those birds which present themselves according to his fancy, and neglecting the shots he finds difficult, which are obviously those which he should practise most.

One of the most puzzling shots is the dropping bird which does not move its wings, for unconsciously the movement of the wings assists the shooter in judging the pace at which the bird is flying, and when it is soaring the pace is very difficult to estimate. Lord Walsingham holds that the best way of hitting a bird of this kind is to snap at it as one would at a rabbit, and I am of his opinion. It is easier to judge the speed of a bird's flight after it has passed; but the shooter should always fire at it first as it approaches him, otherwise he loses time, and will never head the list at a big shoot.

When a bird flies high and steadily, the easiest angle is the perpendicular one, that is to say, straight over the shooter's head; but here again, if he waits for this angle he loses the chance of getting a second shot with turning round.

Aiming at the bird's head, and tipping the gun forward at the moment of firing, is sometimes advocated, but I, personally, do not approve of this method. When the bird has passed, the aim must be taken below, and very much below, where it is flying high. This is by no means easy, and the natural tendency is to shoot over, that is to say, behind the bird.

The curling bird, which flies in a half circle, should be aimed at very quickly on the inside curve of its flight, and the gun fired as it reaches the shoulder.

The cross shot, the most useful of all for driving purposes, should be taken well in front, rather above the bird, with a strong swing.

Now *Swing* is one of the secrets of good shooting. The gun should be moved as far as can be judged at the same pace as that at which the bird or beast is travelling. The swing should continue after the charge has left the barrel, just as a golf club or a billiard cue should continue to follow the course which the ball takes after it has been struck. Both eyes should be kept open, the left hand well forward along the barrel, but not so forward as to risk straining the muscles of the back or arms, always taking care not to drop the muzzle at the moment of pulling the trigger; the legs in the position described on the previous page.

When you are placed in a butt or behind a wall, it is very necessary that either should be so arranged as to hide you as much as possible, whilst allowing you plenty of freedom of action.

In the case of a circular butt, it is wise to pull down a good deal of

Shooting 'down the line' or swinging over the heads of neighbouring Guns is one of the most common examples of dangerous conduct. The gun should be dismounted as the bird approaches the line and re-mounted only after it has passed safely behind

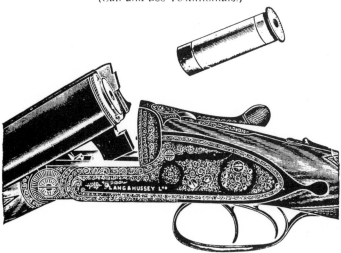

the back part so as to facilitate your shooting at birds which have passed flying low.

In partridge driving, when standing up to a hedge or wall, it is all important that these should be of the right height. They generally require heightening or lowering. Twigs or boughs should be bound down or raised in the hedges, and stones should be removed from, or replaced on, the walls, so as to ensure a comfortable screen for shooting.

I also lay great stress on the importance of keeping quiet during a drive, as birds are wonderfully quick at detecting any movement or sound. People often say to me, 'The birds seem to avoid me and fly over you.' The reason is that I have kept quiet till the moment of firing, while my neighbours have been laughing, talking, jumping about, and really acting as flankers to me. This advice may appear to be of a most elementary nature, but it is remarkable how often the simple precaution it advocates is disregarded.

I will conclude these few remarks on the *technique* of shooting, which I proffer for what they are worth, with my favourite maxim: *'Aim high, keep the gun moving, and never check,'* for it is one which has proved immensely serviceable to me all through my life. I cannot, however, dismiss the subject of shooting altogether without alluding to that side of it which appeals so strongly to every true sportsman, and that is the close contact into which it brings him with nature. To be really interested in shooting means a knowledge and study of woodcraft, of the habits and ways of bird and beast. The legislation which is levelled against the owners of land is doing its best to destroy the old type of country gentleman in whom the love of sport and nature has always been indissolubly united. To him the crow of the grouse as he speeds along the purple heather, or the guttural note of the pheasant as he flies across the crimson sky on a winter's afternoon brings with them a sense of joyous exultation; and the moors, fields, hedgerows, and woods, sheltering myriads of winged and four-footed creatures, are for him full of potential and indefinable charm.

Maybe a generation will spring up to whom all these things will be a closed book; but when that day comes England will lose her most attractive and distinctive feature, and one of her most cherished traditions. For the England of whom the poets have sung for many centuries will have ceased to exist.

Reprinted from *King Edward VII as a Sportsman,*
by Alfred E. T. Watson, Longman, Green & Co., 1911.

Thus the words of one of the greatest game shots of all time, and still they hold good, although the opportunity to use trios or quartets of guns is not an everyday occurance.

In those days the British firmament was full of shooting stars, but they had had their day: one by one they fell, for this reason or that, and a new era of field shooting dawned. Between the wars the great estates carried on much

as before, and rough shooting and even modest driven shooting came within the orbit of the middle classes who now had a little more money and leisure time; and it was considered no bad thing to walk in the steps of the aristocracy.

World War II intervened to put a stop to most of it. Shotgun cartridges were strictly rationed and unavailable for most of the time. Keepers and gunsmiths went to the wars and estates fell into disrepair as we were all more preoccupied with growing food and fighting a war than with our shooting. Post-war austerity meant little change and the best English shotguns could be bought for a song; many things were still in short supply and game shooting remained in the doldrums, although the great estates seemed to be proof against the worst that fate and recession could throw at them.

The quiet revolution began sometime in the sixties. A new era of prosperity was on the way, and thanks to the New Age magazine writers, wildfowling became universally popular and shooting of all sorts returned not only to fashion but to general popularity. The trend gathered momentum and where once the sport was the preserve of the aristocracy and typified by the hungry pursuit of huge bags, suddenly owning and using a shotgun became as popular with the man in the street as golf. Imported guns from Spain were a fraction of the cost of the best English and well within the price range of the new sportsman.

The classic game shoot remained beyond the resources of most, however, and reverted to the rich and famous owners of great estates. Then someone realised that shooting could be sold to those desirous of joining the club but who had no shooting of their own. This idea manifested itself in two ways: in the growth of the syndicate, and the so-called 'let day'. The syndicate comprised a team of keen shooting men who rented an estate and engaged a keeper and ran it in the tradition of the bad old times. They had their own driven days, and relearned the lessons of Ripon; they also learned to appreciate the great arts of shooting flying birds and showing good quality ones. Such folk were often businessmen made wealthy by the new prosperity of the age, and the money they injected into the sport did nothing but good for keepers, gunsmiths, cartridge makers (ie Eley) and farmers.

The quality and size of a shoot was governed entirely by cash, and modest set-ups cost less than ones where rearing on a grand scale continued. Time passed, and shooting suddenly became socially valuable; there was also a hint of a return to the greed and lack of sportsmanship sometimes found in the old days. You could pay by the day or by the bird shot. Sad to say the business attracted some unscrupulous businessmen and some shooting men who would have been better off staying at home. Seller and buyer deserved each other, and they did the sport nothing but harm.

It took another recession to weed out the worst of both worlds, but it left the shooting field a healthier place. Quality shooting remained on the well kept estates, good syndicates flourished, and the quality of the countryside improved most where shooting was strongest. The influence of the Game Conservancy played a significant part in the revival. It showed how game birds could be increased most effectively, and how the whole quality of the British native habitats could be enhanced. The proper ingredients in food for delicate chicks, how to farm with game birds in mind at little cost to the cropping, how to create kindly environments from nothing, and how to run a shoot if an amateur: all these were within the GC remit.

There can be few shoots in the country today where the Game Conservancy's influence is not felt, even if indirectly. Moreover, there is no reason why any citizen who is entitled to hold a shotgun certificate might not shoot driven game, sometimes at some of the legendary covertsides made famous by the Victorian stars. As in most things, you get what you pay for; but it is true to say that field shooting has never been more popular as a sport, with just under one million citizens holding a sporting shotgun.

The shooting scene in Britain today is the envy of the world, and for that reason many foreign travellers come here every year to enjoy our shooting. The man of means might start with the red grouse, shooting in Yorkshire or Scotland, standing in a butt to shoot them (at horrendous cost) or walking them up over dogs (at a fraction of the price, but rather more tiring). In September he might come south and shoot driven partridge in Hampshire or Norfolk. Redlegs are common enough, although the native grey partridge has fallen on hard times. Reared redlegs make up the bulk of most partridge shooting today, and good sport they make. He might flight the mallard on the stubbles in the meantime or have a few shots at the clay ground to keep his eye in.

Then the pheasants would be the main theme. On shoots large and small—from those with numerous keepers and large rearing programmes, to the small set-up on a bit of farmland which a group of enthusiasts seeks to improve by their own efforts in their spare time—the lucky man will find his diary full. If he be true sportsman, he looks for the challenge and thrill of shooting hard and fast birds and shuns those places where the bag is still all-important. In January he goes on cock shoots to thin out the birds surplus to the breeding season. He may pay for his shooting by the day; be invited by friends; or be a member of a syndicate, in which case he invites guests who are expected to invite him back; or he may himself work at running a little DIY shoot of his own. The possibilities are endless.

He would do well to recall that the driven shooting he enjoys today was first 'discovered' by those curious Victorians who, backed by a developing gun trade, by keepers who knew their business, by the railways and royal patronage, proceeded to put their sport on the map of Britain where it has stayed for a century. The fact that there is more of it now and that it is more popular than ever is a tribute to the Walsinghams, Stoners and Co who showed the way.

2
The Quarry

Those birds which may be pursued legitimately today are the survivors of a long line of quarry species. In medieval days almost anything could be taken and nothing was protected. Edicts were sent out positively to encourage the destruction of kites and ravens and others of today's rarities, and anything with a scrap of stringy meat on its bones would certainly be eaten by somebody. The creatures of genuine venery included herons which were hunted with hawks, great bustards (now extinct), and a list of game birds not that far removed from those we pursue today. The pheasant was rare until this century and the rearing programmes and new agriculture which gave it a boost. The grey partridge was common, the woodpigeon infrequent, the swan fair game if you were royalty or a member of the Vintners and Dyers Company in London. Wildfowl of the eastern counties were taken in great numbers in decoys, and bought and sold at Leadenhall Market. Snipe and woodcock were caught in horsehair nooses or 'springes'. The population— or lack of it—of most game species depended almost entirely on the type and level of agriculture prevalent at the time and in the particular area.

Subsequent centuries of pursuit have resulted in game either becoming extinct or close to it (such as the corncrake and quail), or placed on the list of protected species. Recent additions to that catalogue include, among others, the curlew, redshank, stock dove and brent goose, although these birds are of more interest to the rough shooter than the game Shot; however, I make the point to show that no game species is safe from legislation. Curiously enough it is the shooting fraternity who can be relied on most often to protect dwindling stocks, for the motive of self-interest is a strong one.

There are three principal species of interest to the modern game Shot, and it is proper that he should know as much about them and their habits as possible. These are no animated clay targets covered in feathers, but real creatures. The opportunity to shoot one is a privilege not to be taken lightly; the chance to shoot a bagful on a driven day is a rare gift indeed. As well as dressing up properly for the shooting day, being suitably skilled in the noble art of shooting straight, and making sure you are equipped with the proper hardware, you owe it to the quarry to have immersed yourself in an understanding of its habits and lifestyle.

The red grouse is generally accepted as the fastest and most tricky game bird that flies. A bird of the heather moors, it skims the contours, uses every up-draught and explodes over the butts in a way to set the pulse racing. A red grouse well retrieved by a black labrador is a sight which remains forever fresh in the memory

The three birds of principal interest are the grouse, which lives on heather moorland mainly in the north of the country; and the pheasant and partridge (two species), which inhabit the easier climate and agricultural heartland mainly of the south and east. The latter areas are favoured by a kindly climate with warm, dry summers and cold, dry winters; however, being flat, they tend to show birds less favourably—counties to the north and west being more hilly lend themselves to showing more difficult and thus more sporting birds.

Habitat is all-important, and a farmer who wishes to enjoy or let out his shooting must quickly realise that a prairie farm without hedges or trees (because he has ripped them all out in the sixties in order to squeeze in a bit more barley that nobody would ever eat) will never hold game of any sort. So, those who wish to harbour game must remember lessons learned long ago: that good habitat is essential, so cover crops should be planted—mustard, kale, maize, texel greens, artichokes, stubble turnips and others—and woods and spinneys established in likely places. The Victorian great estates knew well enough that game would not flourish without suitable harbourage.

The Red Grouse

Revered by many as the king of gamebirds, the red grouse has much about it to intrigue and fascinate. Living as it does in the most hostile terrain and subject to the most inhospitable weather these islands has to offer, the grouse is unique to the United Kingdom, although various sub-species live in other parts of the world. Little can be done to help it, and the grouse-moor keeper is not condemned to the slavery of either the rearing field or the water-carrying chores of his southern counterpart. The grouse feeds almost

exclusively on the shoots of heather, apart from the first few weeks of its life when, like all game birds, it depends on protein-rich insect life.

Heather tends to grow well enough by itself, and all the moorland manager can do is burn it in rotation to ensure a good supply of fresh young shoots and not too much of the old, woody stuff which is good for shelter but little else. Some moors are short of grit which all birds need for their digestive systems, and this has to be provided by hand; but apart from keeping down the vermin, the grouse keeper's work-load might be viewed with envy by the man from Norfolk. Large-scale poaching of grouse is almost unknown, for the birds roost or 'juk' out in the heather or cotton grass and not in trees like the silly pheasant. The worst that can happen is that some brave rascal walks another man's moors in broad daylight for a few brace, which does little harm apart from the disturbance.

The enemies of grouse cause a problem to the moorland keeper. Protected birds such as the peregrine, golden eagle and hen harrier can cause great disturbance and take many grouse chicks while feeding their own young. There have been unfortunate cases of keepers taking the law into their own hands. It is easy for absentees to pontificate, but nonetheless there ought to be room for uneasy co-habitation, and especially in glut years the predations of raptors are comparatively light. The penalties for any keeper taking protected birds is severe, and steps are being taken now to make the landowner responsible also.

The best thing that the moor folk do is preserve a delicate and valuable habitat. If there were no heather moor, all the eco-systems would vanish: the lizards, pipits, frogs, snakes, merlins, butterflies and bees which interdepend in that very special place. There are great financial inducements for those who plough up moorland and plant desolate miles of conifers which as a wildlife habitat are all but useless. However, as long as great landowners—and I cite the Earl Peel of North Yorkshire as one of the most

distinguished—are prepared to make the sacrifice in order to preserve the shooting, then these magical places will be saved for future generations.

The game Shot does not walk up his birds but has them driven towards him, in the usual format of a team of beaters armed with flags pushing them in from a great tract of heather. Grouse beaters need not be as close together as pheasant beaters since the birds are easy to flush, especially in wet weather when they are up on the heather keeping a lookout. In very hot conditions and where the heather is old and thick they take a little more shifting, and a few dogs might be useful.

The guns are placed forward in a line of butts made of stone or wood. The placing of the butts is critical, although they have probably been in the same place for a century or more, since the driving of grouse began. The contours of the hill and the lie of the best land will dictate where they are, and generations of keepers and moor managers will know what to expect. The approach to the butt might well be over rugged country; some will walk it, but this takes a deal of shooting time out of the day, and it is hard going for the senior members. On most moors transport will be provided in the form of all-terrain vehicles such as the Argocat, with the last few hundred yards being done on foot. Time was when ponies were the only moorland transport available; they either carried the kit—and when we note the huge bags made in the early days the sheer weight of cartridges alone must have been considerable. Some grew adept at shooting from horseback.

Butts are designed to blend with the background and the best are creations of real craftsmanship and beauty; topped with turves and each with its own drainage system, they amount almost to miniature, roofless cottages. The Gun and his loader take their places in one of these palaces and gaze forward at the shimmering heat dancing over the miles of purple bloom. To right and left are the butts of their neighbours, and the Gun will note their positions carefully. Driven grouse tend to fly low, hugging the contours, and often pass at head-height between two butts. Great care and self-discipline are therefore essential in this form of driven shooting, and accidents are not unusual even with experienced practitioners: sometimes tall canes are jabbed into the ground at either side of the leading edge of the butt to prevent a Gun following through and shooting down the line, which is a cardinal sin. Birds which have passed by may legitimately be taken behind, but only after the gun has been dismounted and realigned after the birds have gone through.

The waiting is an exciting time. Far off a whistle might shrill, for the beaters are still miles away and out of sight over the brows of numerous intervening hills. Just ahead a host of black specks falls and rises, you heft the gun and find that you are about to take aim at a cloud of gnats or bumble bees. Grouse can make you behave like that. Nerves on edge you wait and wait, for drives can seem to take an age before the action starts.

Then there is no doubt: no gnat or bumble bee this, as a single grouse with a throaty cackle 'go bec bec bec bec . . .' comes from far ahead frighteningly fast, and straight at your head. You remember well all the good advice to take it far in front, but as you mount the gun at extreme range, blot out the bird and prepare to fire, you see it over the gun barrels going like steam, the fastest game bird that flies, and with just a hint of a curl or sideways swing it is over you and past. No fear of shooting down the line, as it is gone from you before you can turn round and re-address it.

You have to be very quick and alert. The next whistle heralds a large pack, but this time you are ready for the speed and are able to select a slightly easier chance at a bird which flares across your front—and you drop it to bounce along the heather with a squirt of white feathers as it falls. Your second one falls within a yard of it and you feel a good deal better. If you are in the 'A' team with a loader you will change smoothly, and if the Gods are with you, you will take a second brace in the style of the masters of Lord Walsingham's day—and you might find yourself thinking about his 1,070 grouse shot on his own in one day, and wonder what sort of superman could have accomplished such a feat. The thrill of shooting driven grouse remains as potent as ever it was, and the bird has a special magic never to be forgotten by those who have been lucky enough to find themselves in a grouse butt.

The game Shot may quite legitimately take part in walked-up shooting which takes him to the wild places in pursuit of the famous bird, but nothing quite beats the driven article. Later in the season in bumper years grouse shooting may be bought quite cheaply: the red grouse suffers peaks and troughs of breeding success so that in some years they will pass over the butts two hundred strong, whilst the following season might be seen only in half-dozens. It is one of the ironies that this most expensive bird to shoot will die by Christmas unless it has found a defendable territory for itself; and in a fat year this will be less likely than in a lean one. Thus late in the year the moor owner is keen to thin his stocks to a good breeding level, and usually there is little hope of doing so, no matter how hard they are shot. He who bides his time and watches the advertising columns of the sporting press will therefore be able to buy good driven grouse shooting at a fraction of the cost of early season birds.

To find out more about this bird I recommend two books by the same author, Brian Martin, sometime Features Editor of *Shooting Times*: *Sporting Birds of Britain and Ireland* and *The Glorious Grouse*. Both of these study this fascinating bird in depth, and he who takes himself to the high moors in pursuit of it denies himself much pleasure and a new dimension to his sport if he travels ignorant of the natural history of the most famous game bird in the world.

The Pheasant

The pheasant arrived on these shores during the Roman occupation as a table bird, and has become the principal quarry species of the modern driven game shoot. Down the centuries it has been revered as a sporting bird, and deemed delicious to eat by successive generations of the great and the good. In the days of Henry I you needed a special licence before you could take one, the goshawk being the most efficient method of doing so in close country. A bird killed by a hawk was more valued for the table than one

killed by other means, the flesh being said to taste sweeter. In 1170 St Thomas à Becket was said to have dined off pheasant the night before his unfortunate end. For countless years, recipe books and household manuals have featured the pheasant heavily, though in fact it was found almost exclusively in only the best houses.

Henry VIII proclaimed game preserves in Islington, St Giles, Hampstead and Highgate—though today you would walk many a weary mile in those places before you saw a pheasant's feather. King James imposed the first close season, Queen Elizabeth I established fines for night poaching, and one way and another the gaudy and silly bird imposed its presence on the tapestry of British history. Then, as now, it must have displayed considerable powers of survival in the wild, for life must have been difficult in a countryside swarming with predators and lurking fowlers with their 'croce bow, hand bow, dogges, halkes or girnes in the king's haill wooddes, Forrestes and Parkes'. No record of pheasant coverts as such or rearing appear in the early times and it seems likely that the pheasant was almost entirely a wild bird and took its chance.

In 1762 a law was passed which made the taking of a bird outside the close season illegal, unless it were for the purpose of keeping it in 'any mew or breeding place'; thus it is known that by the mid-eighteenth century pheasants were caught up alive and kept, but for what purpose is uncertain.

In the nineteenth century rearing was in full swing, though in the early years the walked-up bird was the main target. The early start to pheasant shooting (1 Oct), at a time when many birds are scarce full grown, is a relic of those days, because if you left it too late the poults had grown too strong and too wary to be approached easily, and your stock was lost to you. 'Get your bird early' was the motto, preferably before it strayed onto your neighbour's land. Another point to remember is that the woods of those days were dense and ill-managed, nothing like the tidy little spinneys we have today with their rides and open spaces neatly cut. Once a pheasant wandered into a stretch of the remaining medieval forest with which the country was peppered, even in the nineteenth century, you never saw it again.

Rearing game for shooting is a recent development and it is thanks to that practice that we have any pheasants at all. Trial and error led to the lesson that in managed woods pheasants could be kept and driven out on a shooting day. The theory was that the reared ones would congregate and mingle with their wild cousins. However, the quality was varied and could be poor, and it wasn't until the first few years of the new century that the great arts of rearing and showing testing birds matured.

It became the norm to cram the woods as full of birds as was possible. New strains were coming in all the time, the black or melanistic, the pale Bohemian variety, and the small, green Japanese all interbreeding freely with the original ring-necked English bird. It might be that, like the British race itself, this new blood was all to the good and strengthened the genes by introducing new lines and with them the qualities of survival. Keepers came to recognise qualities in the sub-species—the Japanese black-neck was supposed to be a good 'stayer' and not stray; the melanistic often grew to great size; and so on.

Pheasants which are some way departed from reared stock and deemed 'wild' were, and are still, highly sought after. The little pheasants from our Fenland are a case in point, half the size of a reared bird, wiry, cunning, excellent fliers and good mothers. Estate birds tended to grow fat and lazy and it takes nothing less than a gale of wind for them to rise above the trees. Those with stocks of wild birds were said to have erred if they introduced reared pheasants just to swell the bag in the short term because the new and poorer blood would dilute the wild strain and reduce the sporting quality of the whole pheasant population on the shoot.

In order to show the game Shot the best pheasants, the keeper takes advantage of the natural undulations in the land. The trick is to persuade the pheasant to fly high when its natural inclination is to do as little work as possible to get from A to B: it would far rather walk anyway, given the choice. The pheasant may be fed regularly to some outlying spot away from home so that when flushed it will fly back. If that flight-line crosses a valley or line of tall trees which needs to be negotiated, then the bird will fly high and the sport will be good: a good keeper and shoot captain takes this into account when planning the drives and placing the pegs. On established drives the decision is as good as made in advance—like grouse butts, the pegs have been in the same places for more than fifty years.

A pheasant is very much a sprint expert in the bird world, spending no more than a few minutes per day on the wing, unless disturbed by beaters. Then it explodes in a fury of thrashing wings, accelerating like a rocket to great height and speed, until finally it glides down to some distant haven. The gurus of the Game Conservancy have estimated that a pheasant drains its energy reserves in only eight seconds of flight, and then the gliding phase must take over.

The modern trend of rearing has changed. All pheasants are inveterate strayers, and reared birds are marked with tags so that returns may be assessed; these show up at no better than 40 per cent of the bag even on well keepered estates. In some places where freak conditions prevail, better is possible; but rearing is a costly and wasteful business unless one has the manpower available, as in the Golden Age when teams of men and boys could be deployed to do no more than prevent pheasants from straying. The view today is to rear fewer and put more money and effort into improving the habitat. The wild bird is by far the cheapest.

The pheasant would find it hard to survive without the interest of the shooting community. Prey to the weather in the nesting season, easily predated and dependent on insects for the first few weeks of its life, and subject to various diseases (especially when reared in large numbers), it would certainly suffer were the commitment of the shooter to be removed.

The season opens in October—as already mentioned, a relic of the old, walked-up days—but in reality serious pheasant shooting does not get under way much before November when the leaf is off the trees. The birds are driven by teams of beaters, sometimes with spaniels, from the cover and over the guns. Where large numbers of birds are present, beating is a real art, for the object is not to show large flushes passing the guns at the same time—even with a loader the game Shot has but four chances. The birds will sometimes sit tightly and every scrap of cover has to be beaten out to ensure that none is walked over. The ideal stand is one on which birds are flushed gradually and give a chance to all the Guns.

When wounded, the pheasant will run and 'tuck in' to some dense patch of cover behind the line. Pickers-up are on hand to make sure that these 'pricked' birds are retrieved. (Beating, picking up and how to conduct oneself at the peg are covered elsewhere in this book.)

At the end of January it is customary to shoot only cock pheasants, sparing the hens for the breeding season: the pheasant is a polygamous bird, one cock holding a harem of hens. This practice is most significant on wild bird shoots, for not all ground is able to support natural populations; in some places 100 per cent of the stock is artificially reared, in which case cocks and hens may be shot until the end of the season. Elsewhere hens are the seed corn for the future, upon which next season's shooting depends.

The pheasant is as popular on the table as it was in Roman times, though it eats better if hung for a while before preparation. Strung up by the neck in a cool, airy place, out of the sun and beyond the reach of cats and dogs, a brace of birds will keep for at least a week and for much longer in frosty conditions. The hanging allows the fibrous meat and sinews to soften and the gamey flavour to develop.

The pheasant remains the lynchpin of all low-ground shooting, although a recent trend to rear red-legged partridges has taken place. Many farm incomes, game farms, suppliers of equipment, and gun- and cartridge-makers depend upon the pheasant.

Partridge
Grey and Red-legged

The Grey Partridge

The grey or English partridge was the original quarry bird of the country squires of the eighteenth and nineteenth centuries, and upon it was the world of game-shooting first built. It flourished in the wild and weedy fields and the overgrown hedges of horse-based agriculture, in the long stubbles and leisurely pace of Agrarian Revolution farming. 'Mad' Jack Mytton of Helston would shoot a hundred grey partridge to his own gun before lunch—and that in the day of flint and steel. Col Peter Hawker was the partridge man par excellence as well as a wildfowler and he would gallop down the covies, dismount and get off a double shot with his 'Old Joe' Manton percussion gun as they fled: if his diary is to be believed he rarely missed.

Record bags of over a thousand driven partridge in a day were shot at the great East Anglian estates such as Six Mile Bottom, Holkham and Elveden; Hampshire, Yorkshire and Staffordshire were also prominent, but even on

smaller partridge manors, teams of Guns would think nothing of bags of three or four hundred—and to shoot that many you have missed as many and seen as many more. The bird positively swarmed, and lent itself to being walked up early in the season and driven thereafter. The covey would be pushed towards a tall hedge behind which the Guns stood, some yards back but out of sight of the approaching birds. Led by an old cock the birds would top the thorns, see the Guns, and like an exploding star shell would burst in all directions taking evasive action. This was deemed the cream of the sport, and challenging shooting.

The keeper sorts out a bag of red-legged or French partridges at the end of a drive. Less popular than the native grey partridge, the redleg has a preference for running rather than flying, and having flown will not fly again the same day. Wags of a century ago named the bird the 'Frenchman' after its habit of running from the Guns

When it came, decline was swift and emphatic. From as recently as the 1950s the bird has decreased steadily, the reason being modern agricultural practices: hedges grubbed up where partridges used to nest, the land soaked in poisonous chemicals, the destruction of the insect larvae on which the grey is entirely dependent for the first few weeks of its life, and stubbles ploughed in the moment harvest is over. The grey partridge has been adopted by the Game Conservancy as its emblem, and it is a good choice, for no bird reflects so well the state of health—or lack of it—of the countryside. In Scotland the grey seems to have survived better than in the more intensively farmed south.

Rearing has been tried and with some success, although it can be a chancy business since the birds will sometimes pack together in one enormous covey and migrate from the estate for good. Where they go remains a mystery, as one never hears of sudden influxes of partridges, only that they have departed.

The old partridge keeper possessed the genuine skills of his craft, beside which those of a modern pheasant keeper pale to insignificance. He found and noted every nest, marking its position on a map: he protected it from all predators, real and imagined, noted the hatch and number of chicks, and kept a daily eye on them until shooting day. In the vital few days which marked Royal Ascot two small patches were worn bare on his bedside rug: these marks were made by his knees as every night he prayed for dry weather, since not only was that particular week prone to summer thunderstorms, it was also the time when his precious partridges hatched.

Today the grey is not rare, but it *is* a pale shadow of its former glory; for all the research and habitat improvement which has been done, it remains perilously on the edge. There are still those occasions on an otherwise normal shooting day when from far-off comes a rusty chirrup like a church key grating in a lock, and with a heart-stopping dash a covey is up and over you just like in the great days gone by. Harder to hit than all but the highest pheasant, five times as testing as the redleg and certainly on a par with red grouse, if you can bring a couple down your day—if not your season—is made.

The future is uncertain, but a more enlightened approach to conservation, the appearance of 'set-aside' land and more caring landowners, backed by the research of the Game Conservancy hold out the best hope. It is just possible that the countryside has been blitzed too effectively and for too long and that the grey English partridge, the crown prince of game birds, has fallen below the level from which recovery is possible. It will be a black day should it ever dawn, and the British countryside will be a sadly diminished place: and let it be said here that shooting will *not* have caused the loss, but the theft of the habitat.

The Red-legged Partridge

The red-legged or French partridge is the alternative, and not a very good exchange for the native bird. Introduced from the Continent in the mid-eighteenth century it thrived on the flat dry lands of East Anglia but fared

badly in rougher country, not being found in Scotland. Superficially a similar bird to the grey, the redleg behaves quite differently.

Like the pheasant, it would rather run than fly, and in wet, muddy conditions balls of clay gather on its feet so that flying becomes impossible and it can be caught easily by a dog. Once on the wing it flies straight and true over the Guns and is not that difficult to hit. In a strong wind or over valleys it can be made to perform in a more spectacular manner, and on some estates it is taking the place of the pheasant and injecting a new note of excitement into some rather moderate covert shooting. The redleg will live in the same places as the pheasant and may be shown from stands of cover crops or spinneys. The right terrain is essential to show it to advantage.

It is said that the redleg will fly only once in a day, after which it runs to the nearest cover and hides. The grey partridge, like the grouse, will cross the Guns many times. The old purists would as soon stamp their foot in a redleg nest of eggs as leave it, because it was felt that it competed with the grey. That attitude has changed, but it indicates the antagonism with which the arrival of 'the Frenchman' was greeted. It was called 'the French partridge', by the way, as people maintained its natural instinct is to run away from the guns!

The redleg is here to stay, however, and can be shown well on ground where the terrain is undulating. Like grey partridge and grouse, redlegs have a tendency to follow the contours. It has some advantages over the pheasant, many Sportsmen preferring the 'certain something' of partridge shooting (and redlegs will do if greys are not available), compared with its larger cousin. Redlegs are very easy to rear and they stay put in covert better than pheasants, especially if a call bird or two has been left in the release pen to home them in at night. The redleg does not fly as fast as the grey.

The sight of an odd partridge coming forward on a pheasant day never fails to elicit the shout 'Partridge!' from the throats of a dozen beaters as though this were something special, an event of some weight in an otherwise normal day. It does not carry quite the *gravitas* of a shout of 'Woodcock forward!' but it is enough to excite comment.

The strategy of showing partridge over tall hedges with the Guns standing thirty yards back does not work as well with redlegs as it does with greys, unless there is a gale blowing. The redleg has the habit of flushing in front of the beaters and landing in the hedge bottom between them and the Guns, and it can be difficult to flush it again; and even if you do, it will then fly low between the Guns. One way round this problem is to plant a strip of game cover from which the birds will flush in ones and twos: stand the Guns close to the flushing point, for another habit of the redleg is to pass the obstacle—be it hedge or line of trees—and turn at right angles, and to fly along the front tantalisingly in sight but just out of range. This can lead to dangerous shooting, low over the heads of the beaters, and also to wounded birds which are hard to recover—a pricked Frenchman will be down a rabbit hole and irretrievable in a trice.

Flags are useful in any line of partridge drivers, although their deployment is a matter of skill and experience; it is a mistake for the keeper to issue flags to the raw lads in the team. A flag flicked at the crucial moment will turn birds back into a drive and send them the right way. All partridge driving must be conducted with great delicacy, and there should be no bellowing, banging of vehicle doors or shouting at unruly dogs. The keeper and shoot captain must get their Guns into position and the field surrounded before the birds are alarmed. Grey partridge are much more alert than redlegs and will be aware of impending trouble; they have the knack of leaving the scene early, often taking all the redlegs with them.

After the pheasant, the redleg partridge is the most heavily shot species in the formal shooting field, and is becoming more so as estates turn to them in preference to pheasants. Rearing ensures that there will always be a shootable surplus, but the habitat must be good, vermin controlled and winter feeding provided to ensure continuity and good stocks.

Fringe Benefits

As well as the three main game birds, the game Shot may well come across other quarry species in the course of a shooting day. Duck and geese are not usually on the list, and reared wildfowl and ponds are discussed by Arthur Cadman elsewhere in this book, but there are others.

Woodcock

This bird will appear from nowhere and it never fails to cause great excitement. Migrating to these shores from Scandinavia under the first full moon of November—the 'woodcock moon'—it lands on the east coast and makes its way slowly across the country, gathering in Wales and Cornwall whence many of them cross the Irish sea. That strange, mothy flight, apparently so easy to shoot, yet deceptive and really so difficult, if only due to the madness which the cry of 'Woodcock!' inflicts on men usually sane and rational.

In Cornwall there are shoots devoted entirely to woodcock, and for the rough shooter in the western counties the bird represents a significant part of the bag. In some places it is protected by caring landlords although there is really no need to do this as the species is increasing in number; and being migratory, it is here today and who knows where tomorrow? Fond of muddy ditch bottoms, rotting leaves in oak woods, any shelter where there is soft ground for its probing beak to search for earthworms, the woodcock will spring with a whirring of wings and surprise you.

Great care must be taken when shooting at it, as one moment it is high and safe, the next with a flick of its wings and an aerial tumble, it is down and dangerously close to neighbouring Guns or where the beaters are approaching.

To hit a woodcock is a matter of pride, and a thrill of which I for one will never tire. Once shot, the pin feather, the last tiny feather on each wing (sometimes called 'pen' feather due to the esteem in which it is held by artists for its usefulness in painting fine lines), should be removed by the shooter and kept as a trophy to be stuck either in the hat band or, better still, in his shooting diary, which I urge all sportsmen and women to keep. Admire the hundred-and-one shades of brown in the plumage, and that liquid eye; and eventually its supreme excellence on the table: woodcock is eaten with its innards or 'trail' intact.

The woodcock is the cherry on the cake on any shooting day. And if anyone is lucky or skilful enough to shoot a right and left at 'cock in front of two witnesses, he qualifies for membership to the exclusive Shooting Times Woodcock Club; he will also receive a badge, a tie and a bottle of something cheering, together with the right to attend the annual club dinner.

Snipe

Smaller cousin to the woodcock, the snipe loves marshy places, but not the enclosed land preferred by the larger bird. It rises easily and zigzags away with characteristic flight and unmistakable 'scaape' of alarm, making the hitting of one no mean feat. It would be my guess that rights and lefts at snipe are even more uncommon than those at woodcock. This small wader is usually the prerogative of the rough shooter as it gives good sport walked up. However, there are some places where special marshes have been reserved purely as snipe drives. I know of one in Anglesey and another in South Devon where Guns stand behind lines of butts strategically placed and snipe are driven over.

Like woodcock, two snipe in the hand are referred to as a couple and not a brace.

Occasional

Woodpigeons, black grouse, ptarmigan, golden plover, moorhens and other oddments will feature from time to time in the bag at the end of a driven day. It is not often that they are the sole object of the exercise but they turn up as a bonus, like the woodcock on a pheasant shoot. This is not the book to explore these birds in depth, save to say that the game Shot should be able to identify each one accurately.

The brown hare, the madcap fellow of the broken ploughing and autumn stubbles is as native as roast beef and Mr Pickwick. Suffering from population fluctuations, many shooting men today prefer to let the speeding hare scamper through the line unsaluted. Here she sits in form, snug with her back to the wind and her soft brown fur the perfect camouflage

Ground Game

Rabbits and hares are acceptable as quarry species on the driven shoot, and once were considered very important indeed, especially the rabbit where a day's bag would run into many hundreds. More recently, hare populations have suffered serious fluctuations, and conservationists are anxious about them. Time was when hare shoots were held every spring simply to reduce excess numbers, but they have become rare events now. Hare shooting is not to everyone's taste: it is a large animal and can take a deal of killing—inept shots very often send them away wounded, and this is something which no responsible shooter cares to have on his conscience.

The modern trend is in fact not to shoot ground game at all on the driven day. It is potentially dangerous, as pellets ricochet off stones and sometimes beaters or stops are out of sight in line behind a hedge, or a dog is about to pop out its head from the bushes. My advice to the newcomer is to leave ground game well alone even when permission has been given to shoot at it.

This concludes our rundown of some of the most exciting and challenging birds that fly. All are flourishing, none is in danger, none is likely to be rendered extinct by the shooting man—just the opposite in fact, for the heather moors, rich coverts, long stubbles and snipe marshes remain in existence only because the shooting man has a direct interest in their preservation. All that we shoot is eaten, if not by us then by someone else, and each gamebird shares its man-made habitat with a host of other creatures, from bee orchids to purple emperor moths and badgers.

All the quarry species are flourishing, and as long as the game Shot survives to protect them, they will continue to do so.

Quarry Lists and Open Seasons

The list of what the British shooter may shoot is controlled by a number of different Acts of Parliament. The two most important are the Game Act, 1831 (Game [Scotland] Act, 1832) and the Wildlife and Countryside Act, 1981. The former covers a selection of game birds, and the latter covers all other quarry birds. The open seasons are as follows (dates inclusive).

Grouse	12 August–10 December
Ptarmigan (Scotland only)	12 August–10 December
Blackgame	20 August–10 December
Partridge (redleg and grey)	1 September–1 February
Pheasant	1 October–1 February
Capercaillie	1 October–31 January
Snipe	12 August–31 January
Woodcock (England and Wales)	1 October–31 January
" (Scotland)	1 September–31 January
Coot	
Moorhen	1 September–31 January
Golden plover	
Greylag goose	
Pinkfooted goose	
Canada goose	
Whitefronted goose (England and Wales only)	1 September–31 January except in or over areas
Mallard	below high water mark of
Teal	ordinary spring tides,
Pintail	where the season extends
Wigeon	to 20 February.
Gadwall	
Shoveller	
Tufted duck	
Pochard	
Goldeneye	

The Wildlife and Countryside Act 1981 also lists a collection of birds which are considered pest species and which may be shot all the year round. The 'pests list' is as follows:

Wood pigeon	Carrion crow
Collared dove	Hooded crow
Feral pigeon	Magpie
House sparrow	Jay
Starling	Jackdaw
Herring gull	Rook
Lesser black-backed gull	Greater black-backed gull

3
Waterfowl Inland

by Arthur Cadman

Duck Shooting

A huge variety of duck shooting may be found amongst game shoots: at one end of the scale is the downland game shoot, with at most an odd pond here and there, and no river system; at the other end there are proper duck shoots either in large areas of bog and marsh, or where there are one or two large lake systems. These include the various broads of East Anglia, some of the famous lochs in Scotland, and many lakes elsewhere. In such cases pheasants may be incidental, and the whole organisation of the shoot is based on keeping the area totally undisturbed except on duck shooting days; normally these involve morning or evening flight, carried out when there is a suitable wind and with Guns positioned at fairly wide intervals. Big river systems also provide good duck shooting, especially in hard weather.

In between these extremes there are many game shoots where winter flashes may form naturally, or where flight ponds have been created, or where there are large ponds or lakes from which the duck are driven, usually as part of a pheasant day. Such places often have the numbers of duck boosted by hand-reared duck. There are also large reservoirs which may provide good duck shooting, usually at dawn or dusk.

Grey Geese

Some game shoots are used by grey geese (greylags and pinkfeet) either for feeding by day or roosting at night, and this may provide an added bonus for the game shooters: they might arrange an impromtu drive—which, however, usually fails because unless the Guns are also wildfowlers, they so often show themselves or fail to take proper cover; or they might have a morning, or an evening flight. Here it should be mentioned that it is a grave error to shoot the actual roost. Geese can be intercepted on their way in, preferably on a stormy evening and at a distance far enough away so as not to disturb the geese sitting on the roost. Alternatively they may be flighted off at dawn from positions near the roost itself; or they may be shot on the fields where they are feeding, from hides or well concealed positions, with or without decoys. Restraint should be shown in such cases, either by imposing a bag limit or a time limit, the object being to allow the geese plenty of feeding time after the shooting has finished.

One of the success stories of the decade is that of the Canada goose.
Originally an escapee, it colonised gravel pits and ornamental lakes, feeding
on surrounding farmland in ever increasing numbers. Seen as a pest by some,
it is a fair quarry species and a sporting bird, often flying over during duck
drives

Canada Geese

Very many shoots outside the winter range of grey geese may also contain
Canadas, and it is important that a fair toll of these geese should be taken as
they are increasing fast and do much damage. The same methods as for grey
goose shooting may be employed, but Canada geese are easier to drive—
many will be shot during the course of duck shooting. It is best to use
reasonably heavy shot (No 3 or No 1) for geese.

All geese fly much faster than they appear to be doing, and it is easy
enough for a good pheasant shot to miss completely when a skein of
Canadas comes over his head at no great height! On the other hand, for the
Gun who is successful, but greedy, let him carry back all the geese that he
has shot! Five Canadas will slow him down considerably, and will probably
cripple him if he is a little man with a long way to go.

In the case of geese it is necessary to take an opportunity when it occurs.
The thrilling news 'The geese are in!' means close observation and careful
planning, followed by a suitable ambush.

Anecdote

There is the story of the country parson. One late autumn Sunday he had just entered the pulpit when the verger passed him a note. The parson looked considerably perturbed, if not excited. He stood silent, in deep thought. Then he announced: 'There will be no sermon today, as I have received some serious news. We will just have a short hymn and then I shall bring this service to a close.'

One old lady asked the verger, 'What was the bad news you gave the vicar?' The verger shook his head gravely. 'I'm afraid I cannot tell you madam: very serious, very serious!' But the old lady's nephew slipped back into the church after the congregation had left, and recovered the slip of paper from the pulpit. It read very simply 'The geese are in!'

That evening, just before evensong, the parson was observed sweeping out the vestry whilst the verger, covered in goose down, was just finishing plucking the second of two pinks! There is a right time and a place for everything.

Improving the Stock of Wild Duck

Mallard tend to nest too early, so that when the chicks hatch there is very often neither insect life nor cover; if it is cold and wet, survival will be very low. Knowing this, two steps can be taken to improve matters: all the early eggs should be taken and used for rearing—the parents will lay again and

45

hatch these eggs at a more favourable time; and many young ducklings' lives can be saved by feeding. It is assumed that the pond will have been fed the previous season—when, incidentally, it is important to go on feeding until either the migrants using the pond depart, or the home duck start sitting. By continuing to feed after the season ends, the migrating duck will be in good condition for the strain of their journey (and also the breeding parents will tend to return to the same place) and the homebred duck will also be in good breeding condition.

When the ducklings hatch, the mother duck will take them to those points where they have been fed before. A dry patch should be selected and a ring of sheep netting, say six foot in diameter, is put round it; the young ducklings are fed on chick crumbs within this circle, the crumbs being kept dry by some simple form of roofing. Outside the sheep netting the adults can be fed with barley or wheat.

By this means, both parents and ducklings can get a full tummy quickly, and if the weather is cold and wet the mother duck will return to brooding her young promptly and keep them dry and warm. This should allow at least 90 per cent to be reared.

Needless to say, there will be no ducklings to feed if vermin control has not been efficient. Rats, mink, carrion crows and magpies must be eliminated, and foxes need to be controlled, too.

Making New Flight Ponds

Before making a completely new pond, consider whether any existing ponds and lakes may be improved either by enlargement—especially for shallow areas—or by flattening high banks. Islands are always desirable, and floating islands are not difficult to construct. Duck use them for day-resting and for breeding.

To make a new island in shallow water, or to repair an island worn away either by wave action or by geese and ducks themselves, work is best done when the water is frozen in winter. Soil can be prepared on the bank, or earth and stones packed in sandbags or in fertiliser bags, which are then hauled over the ice on corrugated iron sheets and piled where required. When the ice thaws, the spoil sinks and makes the island, though it may take two winters to complete. This is easier than transporting spoil by boat.

New duck ponds are subject to planning permission and the authority of the local water board. Where amenity is a consideration, grants may be available.

Before creating a new pool, first think over the required objectives very carefully. For ducks only (except diving ducks), a shallow pond is required. However, if the water is pure then trout may be desirable, and they need a water depth of four to six feet in places—so a pond for duck and trout must have shallows and deep parts. Coarse fish do not suit duck ponds, first because the winter fishing season causes too much disturbance, also because they compete seriously for duckling food. They should be excluded or netted out.

Obviously the subsoil and source of water are critical features; porous soil is useless, unless the water table is above the excavated depth. In Scotland one owner decided to extend and deepen a shallow peaty pool. A bulldozer removed the peat and a fine pond was made, a small burn being diverted to fill it. But the pond remained empty of water because the peat had overlain a morain of sandy gravel, and this acted as a colander! So the water-bearing quality of the subsoil is vital. Clay is best. Otherwise a pond will only contain water if the water table is high enough, or the source of water strong enough to exceed any loss by percolation and evaporation.

The PH value is important: for example very acid, peaty water is the least attractive and the stock will require feeding. For trout, either natural or base-rich water is required, as it is for much of their natural food including freshwater snails and shrimps. Spring water is excellent. It is usually clean, carries a higher percentage of minerals (good for pond life), and it will freeze less rapidly.

Alternatively a site for a pond might be suitable where a water course can be blocked to flood the chosen area; or where the pond site can be made and water diverted into it; or where an existing wet hollow or winter flash can be deepened and extended. Many people can assess suitable places by eye, but a level must be used before construction actually begins. A theodolite or dumpy survey is unnecessary: an Abney level will suffice, or a bubble level held to the eye with a pointer to read a scale on an upright held by an assistant.

The design of a new pond is important. There should be islands and bays, and all banks, including those of the islands, should shelve down thus making it easy for small ducklings to get out, and minimising erosion due to wave action and ducks' beaks. Usually spoil disposal is a problem, but making islands will help to save costs because they absorb some of the surplus spoil which can be bulldozed inwards. High banks should be spread outwards, except for the dam.

The construction of the overflow is of vital importance. If the pond is to be emptied, a monk is necessary; otherwise the overflow should be on solid ground, and *not* over the dam. The width must be much greater than the width of the intake stream, so as to take the whole of the greatest possible quantity of floodwater. (If a flood goes over the dam, it is likely that the dam will collapse, and cause immense damage downstream.) The intake of the overflow may need concreting or packing with well set hard-core. Where rainbow trout are desired the overflow must have a grid; but if sea trout run up the stream, there must be no grid.

The base of a dam should be five times its height. Often it is desirable that the dam also serves as a Landrover road, in which case it must be consolidated by the construction machinery. Construction is by machine or by blasting. Machines are either bulldozers—earth pushing—or JCB types which excavate by bucket. On boggy ground a wide-tracked machine is necessary, although JCB's can be operated off mats, but work is slow. A Hymac is an excellent machine.

Blasting a pond is the most exciting method. Dynamite or gelignite is useless since it makes a deep hole about four foot in diameter—ideal for catching some unsuspecting wildfowler, but no good for duck. The basis for excellent, shallow duck-pond creation is prilled ammonium nitrate (the fertiliser) mixed with diesel oil, packed in a fertiliser bag and ignited by fuse and detonator. A circle of such bags, let off simultaneously, will produce a pond with an island in the middle; a double row of bags will produce double the width. Some tidying up by machine afterwards may be necessary. This method is ideally suited for peaty soils. A shot firer holding a valid Home Office licence for the use of explosives must fire the shots, and the police must be informed—and it goes without saying that there should be no windows within half a mile!

The first pond I made by this process was blown on a large bog on an estate in Scotland. The owner unfortunately had only one leg, so he had never been able to make use of the bog; however, his first flight on the pond produced seven pinks—the first geese ever shot on the estate. At the time, the actual shots which blasted out the pond also produced a claim from the nearest tenant farmer for an aborting donkey and ditto wife—though neither event was proved to be related to this excellent duck pond!

All ponds are of value for the variety of wildlife—from dragonflies to newts, grass snakes, water birds, voles and herons as well as wildfowl— which will colonise them. Frog and toad spawn must be introduced.

Anecdote

Another parson, new to country life, asked the local squire if he could watch the duck shoot on Boxing Day. 'Certainly, my good man,' said the squire, 'but you'll have to be at the Hall at 6.30am wearing thigh boots. I'll put you in the butt with our best Shot.' Now the best Shot had celebrated Christmas unwisely. Both he and the parson had great difficulty in wading out to the butt, but in the end they made it.

A big fat mallard came over. The best Shot missed with both barrels and swore 'B—, B—!' This happened for the next three or four duck, until the parson thought it necessary to remonstrate: 'My dear fellow,' he said, 'You mustn't use language like that in front of me! I'd never have come if I'd known you were so foul-mouthed. If the good Lord heard you, you'd be struck dead!'

Just then a pochard swung past. The best Shot pushed the parson aside and fired another useless postman's knock, followed by 'B—, B—! missed again!' Immediately there was a vivid flash—and the parson was struck dead. A deep voice from On High was heard to mutter: 'B—! Missed!'

Flighting Organisation

One of the difficulties in a syndicate game shoot is that there may be only one small flash or pond that the keeper has fed, and there is no room for more than three out of the eight guns. The only solutions are to draw for the three

The standing gun must remain alert throughout the drive

Left: **All shoot transport must be insured and up to legal specifications**

Top: **The tapping of sticks is more effective than undisciplined shouting**

Above: **The flat country tends to produce low birds**

Picking up the oncomer well in front

places or to fix a rota for flighting—or to make more ponds! Often, the difficulty is that the keeper may have a lot of duck coming to several ponds, and it is a lovely rough night—but the 'died-in-the-wool' game shooters do not want to turn out again after a cold, wet day's shooting. They want off home as quickly as possible, each with his brace of bedraggled pheasants!

Sometimes winter floods create ideal conditions for duck shooting. On such occasions, and often in the case of flighting, the shoot captain may prefer to treat duck shooting as a bye-day and not to mix it up with a pheasant or partridge day. In any case duck should not be shot more often than once in three weeks, and this should preferably be under stormy conditions.

Reared Duck

Many game shoots rear duck to provide variety to the bag, as an alternative to pheasants only. For instance, if there is a stock of hand-reared duck and the day happens to be one of very adverse weather—torrential rain, heavy snow or fog—when it would be a mistake to attempt to drive pheasants, a good duck drive before calling it a day will mean that those Guns who have travelled furthest will not have wasted their journey.

However, hand-reared duck can become totally unacceptable as a sporting quarry. Take the following as an example: the Guns stand in a half-moon; the duck swim about quacking; the keeper beats a dustbin lid, and a few duck fly a few yards, then settle again. Dogs are sent in. Eventually the duck pass the Guns knee-high: they circle round at head-height and then flop down amongst the dogs . . . and that is that.

Ideally, hand-reared duck should be put on one pond and fed at another, not far away, so that they learn to fly between the two. When put out on a large lake, they usually learn to fly better, as they can be fed in bays and shallows away from where they were put out. They should be put up and made to fly frequently.

It is most important that the reared duck come from genuinely pure mallard. If the drakes have blue bills or if any have white feathers, their origin is suspect.

Mallard are easy to rear provided they are kept dry. Normally they should be put out at eight to ten weeks, but where just a few are reared to implement a small wild stock, then I believe in releasing them at the point of flying as they will mix better with the wild duck. It should be realised that on small ponds a large number of hand-reared duck will tend to keep genuinely wild birds away; the reared duck become aggressive and territorial to strangers, even though each individual is only one of very many other reared duck, which accept each other. Therefore more than a few hand-reared duck on a flight pond are more of a nuisance than they are worth.

Feeding Flight Ponds

Small tatties (potatoes) make useful duck food after they have been frosted, but normally wheat or barley will be used—though whole maize is not 'stolen' so much by small birds and moorhens. Automatic feeders are available for isolated ponds. It is important that feeding should be balanced against the numbers of duck using the flight pond, since a large amount of surplus food is not desirable.

Feeding sounds easy. Bins or other lidded containers are kept handy, and should be accessible for a Landrover so that refilling them is an easier task. The food is scattered in shallow water and around the margins. However, things do not always work out as intended. Put those duck remaining on the pool away in the afternoon and they may not come back that evening—and then they may return at morning flight and stay all day. So he who feeds must be very observant and use common sense. If the duck still insist on doing the wrong thing, then arrange to shoot them at that time.

It is worth noting that a keeper who does not understand duck can spoil everything by being too enthusiastic: 'Over two hundred came in last night—I watched them. Can't make out why nothing came tonight!' One might well ask: How many duck saw him? How many were put off when he left? I would rather hear: 'I saw a good lot going towards the pool last night—can't say how many, I kept well away.' *That* should foretell a good flight.

During periods of hard frost, any ice should be broken.

Planting

The use of shrubs and trees around lakes and duck ponds is something which needs serious thought. First of all, butts made out of growing vegetation are wholly preferable to artificial ones, and the best species to use are as follows: *spirea salicifolia*—a shrub which will grow well in wet conditions and can be kept clipped at the right height. *Cornus alba* (dogwood) will also grow well in very wet conditions; it tends to be too robust and invasive, but if kept clipped it is very useful. *Lonicera nitida* or *ligustris* (privet) make the best growing butts on dry ground.

Shrubs and trees are also important in the control of flight lines. On a big open lake, for example, the flight line may be on a very wide front, but by planting a double row of poplars spaced 10 foot apart and with gaps 60 yards wide, the flight lines may be channelled through the gaps. Each gap will have a butt in the middle, and wider gaps of, say, about 100 yards will hold two butts, 40 yards apart. The best poplars to use are *P. robusta* and *P. tricocarpax tacha mahaka*. Also, new clones of excellent promise have been developed in Belgium; many nurseries have full particulars and stocks. *Alnus cordata* is another suitable fast-growing tree.

Very exposed ponds may benefit from some shelter on the south-west or east sides. Clumps of sallow are useful, though too much of such cover can be a nuisance. Remember that for morning flight one wants to see the ducks against the earliest light, and for evening flight against the last light; high tree growth may make it very difficult to see duck in a bad light.

Encourage duck by planting varieties they like to eat. For example, duck eat alder seeds, and to some extent the later ripening berries—*cotoneaster frigida*, or *c. cornubia* and *stransvesia*. Although artificial food is more reliable, planting burr reed (*sparganium erectum*) and sedges will provide useful food, especially for teal. Mallard love acorns and will flight to oak trees heavily laden with ripe seed; some oaks around a big lake or reservoir are therefore useful, although it is not really a tree for small flight ponds.

Another reason for planting is amenity: for example, white poplars, red willows, snowy mespilus, berried species, crabs, bird cherry and cherries are all attractive to the eye.

Butts

For shooting duck and geese, well sited, well camouflaged butts are essential. Careful observation is required before they are sited, for wildfowl have very definite flight lines which may vary with wind direction or water levels.

Without doubt, sunken butts are the best. If the ground is dry they may be lined with wood, but if the winter water level is likely to rise above the bottom, the butt should be waterproof—a square tank or a large barrel may suffice—and a lid is necessary. A plastic bucket as a baler is also a necessity in case of accidents to water levels! Next to a completely sunken butt, a half-sunken one with low vegetation around it is good.

Where sunken butts are not practical then the butt should be made out of growing plant species (see Planting p55) or of material cut from near by. Phragmites (Norfolk reeds) make fine butts both when growing and when cut; either way they should be tied in to sheep netting. The usual size for a butt is 4 x 4ft. One of the most common and stupid mistakes that is made when a butt is placed amongst existing vegetation, is to trample around on the outside until the vegetation no longer exists! In such cases the vegetation should be tied into the framework from inside.

A grass skirt makes excellent camouflage—not, I hasten to say, for our eager Gun and his companion, but for the framework of the butt. A length of binder twine is laid out and bunches of rushes, or reeds, or other vegetation are cut and held in position by a loop in the twine every two inches. The whole skirt can be tied round the outside of the butt, and a second skirt at a higher/lower level may be necessary.

Wooden butts last a long time, but they look ugly.

Two important points: first, the top of a butt should not be level. There should be high bits and lower bits, so that the short man does not have to jump off the ground to see if any duck are coming, and the tall man does not project several feet above the level butt—which is excellent for conservation, but not conducive to much of a bag. The second point is that when butts are made, ready for 1 September, they are perfect and as the duck are green, everything favours the Gun. By December the butts have become tatty and the duck are much more educated: everything then favours the duck. To make the contest more equal, all butts should be fully repaired in December and indeed whenever needed.

Butts dug into a bank, if not completely sunk, should have a perpendicular face on the side from which the duck will approach, ie over the bank. It is much easier to hide against a perpendicular face than a sloping one.

When siting butts, advantage should be taken of promontories. A butt beyond the end of a promontory, on piles and approached by duckboards, will be very effective. A row of butts on piles across the centre of a lake, approached by boat, is excellent. Floating butts are useful, but they tend to drift, and I have even known an occupant suddenly stop shooting because he was sea-sick!

Where a flight pond is concerned, a straight Andrews cross is the ideal, assuming there is a place on an island for the middle butt. That will give five butts, of which only three will ever be used at one time, according to wind direction.

On a long narrow pool, say 40 yards wide, butts on the edge on each side should be opposite each other, so that a duck half-way can be reached by both, as long as it is high enough for safety. But where there is a long pond of greater width, the butts should be staggered, Nos 1 and 3 on one side, 2 and 4 on the other: duck shot at from No 1 will tend to veer towards No 2; duck shot at by No 2 will swing towards No 3, and so on.

It is an elementary safety precaution for the host to make abundantly clear which butts are occupied and precisely where they are. Also, the time for finishing must be arranged and each Gun must be able to find his way back in the dark. Flashing torches should not be encouraged.

Planks over ditches should have mouse netting stapled on top to make falling off less likely. I well remember a famous plank over a ditch on a famous goose shoot: I led the way over in the dark, followed by a Norwegian, who was followed by an Italian. Suddenly there was an almighty splash and the air turned blue with comments in a foreign lingo. The Norwegian turned to me, with a big grin: 'I can't speak Italian but I think he's swearing!' On another occasion I myself fell off this plank, to the joy of my companions!

Weather and Tide Conditions

Happy the landowner or sporting tenant who has a pool or lake inside the sea-wall of a shoreline where there are plenty of duck. All he needs is a rising spring tide and a howling gale: as conditions become worse 'out there' the duck will seek shelter, crossing the sea-wall and making for the inland waters. Two Guns suitably concealed will have several hours of superb shooting. Decoys add greatly to the bag.

Weather plays an important part in all duck shooting and the best flights are to be had in stormy conditions. A snowstorm is excellent for making a bag of geese. Fog is unfavourable for duck since they do not like to move much, but geese will lose their bearings and flight up and down the first land they reach at morning flight. Thus great sport may be had by he who owns fields adjoining the shore used by geese.

The moon is very important: duck, especially wigeon, pinkfeet and Canadas flight under the moon. A starlit sky is useless as one cannot see them. Ideally a background of fleecy cloud, or mackerel sky makes a moon flight very enjoyable. However, if geese and duck have moved under the moon, then morning and evening flights will be poor. Heavy overcast cloud will make morning and evening flights more normal.

Rough weather is best for all duck shooting.

Dogs for Duck Shooting

Of course one's own dog and one's own breed of dog is always the best. Normally a game shooter will have the dog he considers best and most suitable for game, and it is unlikely that he will have a second, wildfowling dog—so the game dog must be prepared to tackle water, and to pick up winged duck, too. One can talk all night about the best wildfowling dog. I am a labrador man, and will not easily admit that there are better wildfowl dogs. However, Chesapeak Bay and Newfoundland dogs are unbeatable. Curly-coats, flatcoats, golden retrievers are all good, and springer spaniels can be excellent although their coats sometimes show up too much. Furthermore a big greylag gander, winged, needs a powerful dog to bring it back, and so does a Canada. I shall stick to my labradors!

Ethics in Duck Shooting

Whilst one values tall pheasants as a test of skill, to shoot at any bird which is *too* tall is bad sportsmanship. One of the worst forms of bad behaviour is seen when Guns loose off at geese or ducks which are too high to kill cleanly—more so than any other form of unethical behaviour, except where some reared duck are concerned.

To shoot—massacre—a large number of over-tame hand-reared duck is an appalling way to behave. Anyone who has reared a few mallard on the lawn will know how extremely tame and trusting they become, and probably more unethical behaviour occurs with hand-reared duck than in any other form of shotgun shooting. The true wildfowler regards such shots with contempt. Hand-reared ducks must be made to fly well and to know where they can head for safety. If they just fly round and round one small pond, their demise is as disgusting as their behaviour is stupid.

Nowadays when there is prolonged bad weather a ban is imposed on all wildfowling, and this ban must be observed everywhere even though well fed, hand-reared duck are not affected.

There is yet another situation where a form of bad manners happens all too often: at a flight pond duck are seen wheeling round at extreme range, about to drop in. Then some silly fool looses off, hoping to bring off a spectacular shot—and this fellow really *is* a silly fool, whether he kills or misses—and usually he misses!—because he will have spoilt it for all the other Guns, since those duck will not give anybody a second chance! Again, at morning flight the host will say at what time or from which butt(s) the first shot may be fired: the greedy Shot who fires at the first duck he sees may do great harm. Similarly the man who fires at a duck when geese are dropping in to the next butt: he is not popular, and all others hope he will not be invited again. So too the man who fires at approaching geese when they are not in fair range: let him stay at home for the next shoot.

So there can be unethical Guns—and also unethical dogs: the two often belong to each other. A dog that is floundering about in the middle of the flight is not the most popular. If he is your dog, pretend that he is not—do not stand on top of your butt shouting his name at the top your voice. As likely as not he will take no notice, but all the other Guns will not be as discerning as your dog.

It is also bad behaviour not to know how to kill a wounded duck, or goose, cleanly and quickly. An inefficiently 'killed' one may even escape, later!

Finally, if you are invited to choose a couple of duck or a goose at the end of the day, it is perfectly ethical to look at the tail feathers (at any rate before the late moult) when choosing them.

60

4
Kitting Out

The Gun

The rough shooter can get away with almost anything regarding weaponry provided it shoots straight, fits him and fills the bag. I have used some curious pieces, including what were known as 'farm guns', with rusty barrels, great horns of hammers, cracked stocks, and of doubtful pedigree. Innocent as they were of maker's name, their great strength was that they were easily available; they were also almost entirely lacking in choke and so were all accorded the provenance to 'a good killer'. Single barrels, semi-autos—you name it and it would have passed muster, for the rough day has few of the pretensions of the formal game shoot, which has an element of keeping up appearances and doing the conventional thing: to break the taboos you have to be a very strong character indeed.

There is little option in the gun line, therefore, but to take a conventional double-barrelled shotgun, and an over-and-under or a side-by-side are now acceptable everywhere. The OU suffered from a certain amount of prejudice for many years from the more hidebound game Shots, but the weapon took such a hold and proved so effective—some said better even than the side-by-side—that today it is found on the best estates.

As much cannot be said for the semi-automatic or pump action gun. Invariably made overseas, the semi-auto and pump remains the preserve of our American and Continental cousins and is not yet considered suitable for formal driven game shooting in the UK. The reasons are hard to identify, but unlike the recommended guns, you cannot see when an auto is safe for you cannot carry it broken. Moreover, the idea of being able to have five shots at the same bird rather sticks in the sportman's throat—although recent legislation has meant the number has dropped to a maximum of three cartridges in the gun, except in very special circumstances.

Bore

Therefore a double-barrelled gun it must be, especially if it is for the beginner who must not be the one to flout convention. The matter of bore is personal choice. The most popular by far is the 12-bore, easily available, and the ammunition obtainable anywhere; it has become the gun of the UK sportsman. However, other smaller bores can also be used: there is the 16-bore, though this is so similar to the 12-bore it is not often seen; far fewer were made, and not every gun shop has the ammunition—while your neighbour on the shoot will almost certainly not have any in the event of your running out and appealing to him in an emergency.

Far more popular in recent years and already an established favourite with discerning American and Continental sportsmen, is the 20-bore. This excellent gun is lighter than the 12, can be loaded with an ounce of shot, and is more pointable, but it needs to be used just that bit more accurately. The Shot of long experience who finds he is becoming too good with the 12 often turns to the 20 to provide that extra challenge. The smaller gun is quick, pointable, good for snap-shots in half-light, and capable of bringing off shots every bit as spectacular as its larger cousin.

Once the prerogative of boys, ladies and old-timers on the assumption that their lighter frames could handle it more easily, the 20 has become the mark of the connoisseur and there are some remarkable disciples in the field to prove its worth. Its smaller cousin, the 28-bore, also has its advocates—a good gun for a young girl or boy beginner. Ammunition is available quite easily, and its small load of shot can nevertheless be delivered with devastating accuracy, minimal recoil and no handling problems.

For my money the 28 is the smallest of the 'real' shotguns. There has been a custom, less prevalent now I am glad to say, of starting off beginners with the tiny .410. I have nothing against this little gun *in its place*, which is in the hands of a keeper rabbiting over ferrets, or shooting rats in close circumstances, but to my mind it is no gun for a beginner in the shooting field, since the pinch of shot and the tendency of the gun to string it out in a long squirt of pellets allows no margin for error. To give a raw lad free rein with this gun is to condemn him to disappointment and possibly put him off the sport for good.

However, like most rules even this one may be broken. There are one or two exceptionally gifted Shots who have taken to the double .410 and made it their own. They stand far behind the line of guns as back guns, taking what those forward miss, often at greater range than the 12 and they seem to hit every time. Thus the little .410 can be deadly, *but* only in the hands of no more than ten game Shots in the land—so unless you are lucky enough to be one of them, stay away from it.

Fit

Whatever gun you have, it should fit. It is a mistake to try and cut a dash at the expense of comfort and a fitting gun, and a cheap and cheerful gun which fits you is better than a Purdey or Holland which does not. Good guns are very expensive and I suspect that most of them in the field today are either inherited, or were bought for their owners long ago when they were of rather more lissom proportions. To use grandfather's gun, no matter how noble its pedigree, is to try and wear his suit and look comfortable; it might fit, but only by a fluke.

In fact it is easy to make a gun fit, and the money is well spent. Stocks may be shortened or lengthened or cast-altered, and there is hardly a part of a gun which cannot be changed, except perhaps for the length of the barrels—

and even then you can, in extremis, have a new pair made. To shoot with an ill-fitting gun is to shoot under a handicap.

Care

Take a pride in your gun, and look after it. At the end of every season it should be sent to your gunsmith for an annual strip and clean, at which time scratches, tiny dents and other damage can be repaired. Take a pride in having your gun in perfect condition, not only from a safety point of view but aesthetically.

Travel to the shoot with your gun in a leather motor-case. Most good guns come complete with either the traditional oak and leather type lined with baize, or one of the modern ones made of crush-proof honeycomb fibre. This could well save the gun in the unfortunate event of your having a motoring accident, and will protect it in all but the most severe 'prang'. Wood and metal a gun might be, but it is easily damaged: gun barrels should be treated as though made of glass. New barrels for a 'best' English gun cost thousands of pounds, so why take an unnecessary risk?

On arrival, take the gun from its case and assemble it. For the rest of the day you will take it round in a zip- or strap-fastened slip made of leather and lined with wool or quilted padding. The gun is easily put in and out at each drive, and when you are walking about or on the transport it is protected from scuffs and scrapes or the ravages of the weather and mud. A slip will not be sufficient to protect the gun should it receive a good bash against metal, for example a car door, but it will prevent a great many minor marks which over a season will accumulate and cost dearly to have put right, purely cosmetic although the exercise might be. If you leave the slip at your peg while shooting, try to keep rain or mud from getting inside it.

Have in your motor-case a pull-through and a towel or a handful of oily rags. You will not be able to give your gun a proper clean until you get home, but after a good wetting a three-minute session to wipe down the metalwork and pull through the bores will remove much of the water and dirt—every moment that muck is on there, the gun is at risk of deterioration. The modern acid rain can do damage in a short time if a gun is put wet into a carrying case, even for a couple of hours.

Ammunition

The modern shooter is spoiled for choice in the matter of ammunition. There was a time when some of the imported stuff was decidedly worrying and shot was a lottery, ranging from dangerously high pressure to damp squib. All of that is behind us, and modern methods of production have given us a

Overleaf
Two fine examples of 'best' London sidelock guns, both showing signs of fair wear and tear, but sound for many years to come if well cared for. The London gun was for two centuries the envy of the world of gunmaking and a matter of pride to its owner

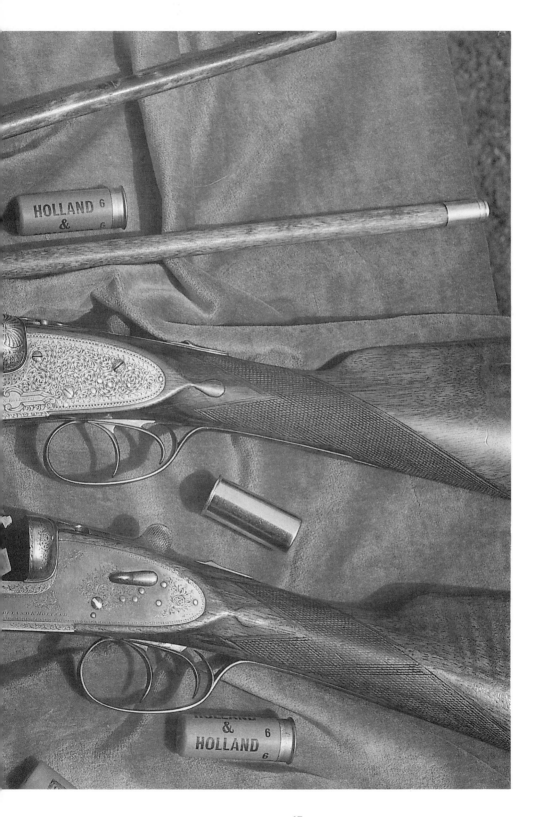

The imported over-and-under shotgun (this one by Beretta) is made to the
highest standards and is fully accepted in the formal shooting field, in spite of
initial suspicion. The 'best' English game gun can no longer claim total
superiority over its continental cousin

wide range from which to choose with confidence. I have tried most of them
and confess to a preference to the ammunition produced by the Hull
Cartridge Company; this I have found excellent and consistent in all ways,
from their wildfowling cartridge to the lighter loads for the covertside. The
reader will find others to his taste and his gun shop will advise.

For game shooting, a light load of an ounce for a 12-bore will do perfectly
well. This should be in shot size 6, 6½, 7 or 7½—in other words, small shot
which in turn produces dense patterns at optimum range. The art of all
shooting is to put a regular pattern of shot within a 30in circle, with the target
its centre—in which case we ought never to miss. Heavier loads are not
necessary, for if you cannot kill with an ounce you will do little better with
any more. Pick up your cases at each peg after shooting; it is a good habit.

Modern ammunition has largely done away with the need for much choke in a gun. Choke is the constriction of the internal bore within an inch or so of the muzzle, which has the effect of holding the shot together for longer and thus providing tight patterns at long range. It is my view that all choke is the invention of the Devil, and that open bores are the secret of full bags. A game gun ought to be bored improved cylinder and quarter choke, ie not very much at all, for most of what you shoot will be well within the maximum range of the gun, and open patterns with small shot form the ideal combination.

Should you decide to take your game gun wildfowling there are cartridges available especially wadded so that the shot stays together for longer without recourse to choke; thus longer-range patterns may be used in an open-bored gun. The day of the heavily choked gun, and people boasting about long-range shots—all flukes anyway—have long gone. Reading old books on fowling can fill the beginner's head with wrong ideas on this subject, and I write as one who knows!

Cartridges should be carried in a cartridge bag of traditional design; these are usually made of leather, and vary in size from about 100 capacity (as many as you would wish to carry), and so on downwards. If you are having a very big day, the bag may be topped up from the spare stocks which will be in the Guns' vehicle and available to you as required. It is the height of bad manners to run out: better to take too many and be prepared to bring them back with you—and once in your life, if you are very lucky, you will need them. Ammunition for immediate use may be carried in the pocket, easily accessible, and many shooting jackets have pockets designed for that very purpose, with button back-flaps and of good size.

There are other ways of carrying cartridges, patent devices which promise this or that, but—and call it old-fashioned prejudice if you will—I have little time for them as no-one has proved to my satisfaction that any of them is better than the bag that has served the shooting man well enough for 150 years. Some use a cartridge magazine of the type favoured by grandfather when he took thousands of rounds on the train with him to the grouse moor. They are handsome things and command a good price at auction, so keep one in your car with your spare supply—but don't expect anyone to carry it far for you; their practical use is strictly limited. If you are fortunate enough to shoot where double guns and a loader are required, the problems of portage are passed on to others.

Ear Protection

In today's world, health and safety seem to have become paramount. In the shooting field the use of hearing protection has become more popular each year, so that nowadays at least half the Guns present on any given day will be so equipped. The corollary is that a distressing number of old and not-so-old shooting men *have* become hard of hearing, or worse. Thus the wearing of hearing protection is surely a small inconvenience to pay for saving one of the most vital of the human senses, and I recommend the practice without reservation.

There are those who claim that although traditional-type ear muffs reduce the violent assaults of gunfire, they also cut out the smaller, important sounds which contribute to the rich diversity and excitement of a shooting day. The chip-chip-chipping of blackbirds as they fly ahead of the beaters, the whirr of wings which gives advance warning of a pheasant's approach, the shrill of a keeper's whistle on a partridge day, the quiet stucatto stutter of mallard, still half a mile off but enough to set the pulses racing—all these are part of the tapestry of a shooting day.

Some of the modern ear protectors are designed to allow such sounds through, yet also cut off the crack of a gunshot. They operate through a system of valves, sometimes worked electronically, so that conversation and small sounds may still be heard. The quality of such reception is not perfect but it is better than nothing, and I still feel that the choice is simple: make that small sacrifice in order to save your hearing in the long term. A deaf, silent and lonely old age is not a prospect which pleases.

The Peg Dog

It is permissable to bring a dog to a driven shoot provided you have made sure that this is acceptable to the host. There might be a problem with transport where Landrovers are laid on, which have room for Guns only and not dogs. The host might have suffered badly in the past from guests with unruly dogs, and is taking no chances. In fact your dog will have little to do, as the pickers-up will gather the runners and dead birds too, while you may pick up the others yourself or a beater will do it for you. However, a dog as company at a peg, and one which will pick up the runner which drops close behind and makes its way off to cover, can only be a bonus. Surely there can be nothing wrong with a dog which adds to the pleasure of a guest's day?

But there is a big if—namely, whether or not the dog is under control, and whether it risks spoiling both your day, or, what is worse, that of others. To have a dog with you which will not allow you to relax because you know it may run in, fight other dogs, or dash off to work out the wood the host was saving for his big after-dinner drive, is to condemn yourself to misery and not to be asked again. The peg dog must sit with you as steady as a stone, without your having to resort to giant corkscrew pinning it to the spot, or lead tied dangerously round your belt, electronic collar or any other artificial restraint. It should stay exactly where you place it and not move a muscle until told to do so, even if dead pheasants rain down tantalisingly close.

Such dogs are rare outside the field-trialing circuit; your trusty hound which has served you well enough for pigeon shooting and working out the rough dykes might be excellent at that job, but it might not suit him to be put under the sort of restraint demanded at a peg; moreover it is unfair to expect it. My advice is that unless your dog is rock steady, leave it at home; and even if it is as good as gold, think twice about just how much you will need it.

Other dogs will be there, and yours could well be a distraction, just something else to worry about when really what you are there for is to concentrate on the shooting and to shoot well.

However, should you decide to take the old rascal, feeling him to be equal to the occasion and provided the host has welcomed the suggestion, take with you a light slip-lead in case you need to go near roads, houses or railway lines; also a towel to dry him out later, a whistle, and a handful of dry biscuits to give him at the end of the day; and finally, make sure that you have in your vehicle a warm and secure place for him as he will be tired at the end of the day. If you are in the big house preparing for your third helping of steak and kidney pie whilst outside there is white frost on your car, do not be surprised if your animal comes down with serious rheumatics before he is middle-aged.

Most peg dogs or non-slip retrievers are labradors or golden retrievers, for they have the qualities of steadiness and good nose which you need.

Incidentals

There are various gimmicks and bits and pieces with which you may, if you wish, festoon yourself. Their usefulness is strictly limited and often the encumbrance outweighs their practical value. For example the shooting stick is redundant for all save the frail and infirm. To see great rollicking chaps, who look as though they ought to be playing rugby league, sitting on a shooting stick, apparently unable to stand unaided for the ten minutes it takes a drive to commence, is a pathetic sight: have they lost the use of their legs?

The shooting stick is useless in soft ground; it also has a habit of banging against your gun barrels and leaving dents in them; and once out of every five times you take it out with you, you leave it behind. It is something else to carry and I can see no sense in it. The exception I have cited is the senior citizen who genuinely finds standing for long periods a trial, and far be it for me to make his life difficult. I bought a shooting stick because I thought it looked good. I used it twice, lost it, found it, used it twice more, lost it again and once more recovered it: now it hangs outside on a peg waiting for me to reach my dotage.

The hip flask is another little accoutrement which can prove a two-edged sword. A wee nip at a cold corner or a flask handed round as part of the bonhomie of the Guns' trailer is fine enough, but it can become habit-forming, the more so if your flask is but one of many present, when you can overdo things. Alcohol and shooting are bad mixers: the human judgement dulled by over-indulgence, combined with a deadly weapon greatly increases the accident potential factor.

Clothing

How you dress assumes some importance on a formal game shooting day: not only should clothing be practical, weatherproof and comfortable with room to swing the arms when shooting, it should also satisfy the conventions of the shooting field. It is not good enough to turn out in your old gardening togs—warm and comfortable they may be, but the true shooter considers it is a discourtesy to the quarry, the host and the beaters to come improperly dressed.

Footwear

Starting with the footwear: not much choice here, and it lies between Wellingtons and leather ankle boots or possibly brogues. The Wellie seems to be the universal footwear of many sporting occasions, easy to put on and take off, proof against wet and mud, providing good protection for the calf and easily available. However, on dry days or on a moor where much walking is expected, leather ankle boots are better, for they provide good ankle support and the feet do not tire when wearing them. The Wellie tends to produce a damp and sweaty foot, leather does not. Leather takes more time to clean and must be lovingly cared for, but leather boots look smart and were standard wear before the Duke of Wellington gave his name to their successor. In wet weather or long grass, however, the leather boot is beaten by the Wellie.

Today there is a compromise. Some firms such as Aigle make a rubber Wellington with a leather lining, either pull-on or with a zip up the side. These are very good; they are fairly expensive, but it is not so bad when you consider that a pair will outlast at least three pairs of ordinary rubber boots. In the field I have also seen old-fashioned long leather gaiters worn with short boots, and there is a shorter variety favoured by grouse moor keepers; they look smart enough and have their advocates but I find them fussy and hardly worth the bother.

Most important of all is that whatever boots you wear they should be well fitting and comfortable, for you will be on your feet for most of the day and nothing will spoil your pleasure more than aching feet or blisters. New boots should, of course, be 'broken in' gradually by wearing them for short periods about the office or along the High Street for a few days, before you give them a full day in the field.

Shooting stockings are worn under them; when you buy new ones, make sure they are long enough to allow a generous turnover at the knee. Several types on the market fail in this respect, and especially after a couple of washes, stretch barely to the garter line even before they have been turned down. The trouble is that they tend to come in sealed packets so there is no chance to check the length, unless you ask that a pair be taken out for your

inspection—nobody buys a pig in a poke! The stocking is a chance for you to express your colourful personality, for they can be had in a variety of hues which look quite striking; I have a preference for the pillar-box red ones.

To keep the socks up it is traditional to use ties with flashes at the knee. These, too, may be in any colour, and use either elastic for support or tie-rounds. The tie-rounds are better as you can adjust the pressure precisely, and thus avoid the constricting effect of overtight elastic. You will also need to take a pair of indoor shoes with you to wear afterwards, or for lunch if the plan is to go into the house. The shoes should be slightly large to accommodate the thicker socks; most shooters have a special pair for this purpose which they keep in the back of the vehicle. A boot-jack is useful and saves much hopping around on one leg heaving at a muddy boot, giving yourself blood pressure and a strained back.

A useful little luxury is a Wellie bag. This is a simple nylon bag which takes a pair of Wellies comfortably and thus keeps the mud off the inside of your car. Muddy boots have a habit of spreading their mud thinly over all surfaces, without human aid. The Wellie bag keeps it all in one place and seems to be one of the slightly more useful developments of the decade. Ask for one for Christmas.

Trousers

Next comes the trouser section, and here breeks or plus-twos are *de rigeur*. Not all are blessed with the legs for them, but breeks have become standard wear and really nothing else will do. Anyone who intends to take his shooting seriously is going to need a pair sooner or later, so why not sooner? The breeks should be of good quality—as in most things, you get what you pay for: a strong Derby tweed, Irish thornproof, corduroy, loden or moleskin are best. The likes of Harris tweed can be a little harsh on the skin, so you need them lined. One firm produces an unusual and excellent breek made from cotton-lined waxproof cloth; these are first class if you are expecting foul weather.

All breeks fasten at the knee, with either velcro, a strap and buckle, or a lace. Take your pick, but those with muscular calves find that the velcro can burst open at inconvenient moments, and it is easy to do up the strap too tight and add too the constriction caused by the garters. Pockets ought to be deep to prevent things falling out; some breeks have pockets which button down. The seat and knees ought to be double thickness, as those are the parts which take most punishment. Belt loops should be generous enough to take a wide leather belt (it is surprising how often this is overlooked), or you may prefer braces. Moleskin (brushed cotton) is the softest material, and is good in fine weather, but the cloth fades after a few washes until it becomes almost white. It might well be that your plus-twos are part of a shooting suit—of which more later—otherwise you buy the breeks separately and opt for a non-matching jacket, carefully selected (see p74).

Like all your kit, your breeks should be kept clean and smart, mud and dirt sponged off after each outing, hung on a hanger, and dry-cleaned each season. A well dressed and smart member of any team is usually an efficient and happy one, and others will notice if you become slovenly.

The Shirt and Tie

The shirt ought to be wool or cotton—natural materials are always better than man-made fibres—in a modest check. Shirts of too bright a hue tend to catch the eye, and the sartorial theme should be one of inconspicuousness; approaching birds will be put off by the flash of white collar and cuffs. It should be fully fashioned with good tail, and generous across the back where you will be stretching and swinging each time you shoot; any constriction there is unhelpful. Keep a few shirts exclusively for the shooting field.

I have changed my view about the neck tie. I have written elsewhere quite passionately in favour of the cravat or choker in preference to the formal tie, arguing that the tie always slipped awry and ended up under one ear, and was generally impractical. But if you cannot beat them, join them: I was finding myself in a minority of one, and as I have been at pains to point out, the shooting field is nothing if not conventional—it does not do to buck the system. Choose a modest tie, preferably one of the Game Conservancy, BFSS, BASC or other national sporting organisation. There is no harm in advertising.

Jumper and Waistcoat

On top of the shirt you need something warm, for you may well be out in the worst the British winter can throw at you, and nothing is more miserable than being cold. The trouble used to be that the warmest middle-layer clothes tended to be bulky, so that when you wrapped up the subsequent loss of mobility made shooting almost impossible. In the old days I favoured a sheepskin flying jacket for wildfowling; this was ideal for sitting in the cockpit of a Lancaster, and cosy enough when crouching in a hide—but just try to swing the arms at a passing, fleeting shadow . . .

Two thin wool sweaters are better than one chunky-knit one. Better still is the quilted waistcoat, now universally worn by all manner of countrymen, which allows the arms freedom of movement while keeping the trunk warm. The theory is, keep the centre snug and the extremities will look after themselves. If you have a shooting suit you have the option of a waistcoat made of the same material; close-fitting tweed is extremely warm and comfortable, but make sure it comes well down the back to keep the lumbar area warm. Many chills result from a lack of protection there.

Accessories

Minor accessories include gloves, for cold fingers do not make for efficient shooting. Full gloves take too long to pull on and off so most shooters compromise with mittens. These take various forms, including the back-of-the-hand covering with warm wristlet, the theory being that warm hands make warm blood which then also circulates to the fingers; alternatively full gloves with the trigger finger cut out are good, provided the leather is fine enough to allow sensitivity of touch. I have found that the handwarming pocket beats all gloves save on the coldest day; any glove is frankly an impediment to good shooting, so if you are able to manage without them, then do so.

A woollen scarf seals the gap between the top coat and the shirt. Warm air positively rushes out of this space and undoes all the good work achieved down below, so a warm scarf is a handy item. It is considered old-fashioned by some, but I swear by one on all but the warmest days.

It is said that up to 70 per cent of body heat is lost through the head, so a hat is essential, and not only for that reason: the human face is a noted bird-frightener, and when turned upwards, peering at approaching birds, it can cause them to swing to left or right. Watch the man without a hat and see that he gets comparatively few shots when standing in open country. And quite apart from its practical uses, a hat is customary. Its colour should match the ensemble and blend with the subdued tints of the British countryside; whether you choose deerstalker, pork-pie, Derby tweed or a cloth cap is a matter of personal preference. Those with peaks fore and aft do shed the rainwater down the back rather than inside the coat collar, so they have much to recommend them.

The Coat

Finally the coat: this is probably the most expensive and most important item of clothing. A good shooting coat ought to last many years with care, and so the choice is important and worth getting right. Any fool can be wet and uncomfortable in the wrong coat on a shooting day but such discomfort is self-inflicted and unnecessary. We are well served, and the early experimental years of trials with India rubber, oilskin and mackintosh have passed, along with Sir Ralph Payne Gallwey's nineteenth-century coat-making tips involving three men in the stable yard, a vat of boiling linseed oil, a linen smock and three days' work.

The ideal shooting coat should be warm, waterproof, not too heavy, well-fitting, with adequate pockets for personal possessions and a button-up flap for easy access to cartridges. It should breathe, look smart, have storm collar and cuffs, stout zips, in a perfect world no pop-on studs, and be blessed with that vital, hard-to-define ingredient which makes you feel good when wearing it.

To keep warm and dry today is easy: you invest in a Barbour Solway Zipper waxed cotton jacket (recently adopted as smart wear for Sloanes); my old Barbour lasted for years, and in its day the Barbour was—and is still—the almost universal topcoat of the shooting field and on many other sporting occasions. It became so popular that the very word Barbour has passed, like the mackintosh it replaced, into the language as a common noun. There were times when every Gun and beater wore one.

Its rugged practicality includes storm collar and cuffs, a welter of practical pockets, uncompromising resistance to wind and rain, and a hood with studs; it is also barbed wire resistant, and backed by the best coat repair service in the world. All this has made the waxproof essential kit for three generations of shooting folk.

However, nothing is perfect and even the Barbour has its shortcomings, some of which its owners have come to love as they might a rascally errand boy. The cloth does not 'breathe', and so the perspiring body, warm from a walk, makes the lining and then the shirt as wet as though from a downpour. The wax proofing of the cloth wears thin at key places, notably the shoulders and crooks of the arms, and lets in the rain; and when newly oiled, the coat leaves a thin layer of grease on all surfaces, especially car upholstery. The colour of the cloth changes quickly from olive-green to black as more and more dirt becomes ingrained; when cold it is as stiff as a board, when warm it smells and feels like a wet dog.

For all that, we still loved our Barbours and, at the time, accepted its weaknesses as fair exchange for its towering strengths; there was no coat like it on the market then. But in time we became pernickity and expected more: where was the coat which not only kept the rain at bay, but also *breathed*? One that looked smart, and did not become like an old sack? Manufacturers tried this and that, but with moderate success and great expense, and we hurried back to our waxproof with something like relief. The advance of science could not be denied: if we could put a man on the moon and bring him home again, surely we could make a coat that breathed?

Courtaulds developed a yarn spun from long-staple cotton, doubled for extra strength and lightly proofed. The secret was that when wet, the fibres expanded, allowing the micro-sized droplets of body vapour to vent out whilst keeping at bay the much larger molecules of rainwater. They called the new material 'Ventile' and it had a tough testing on the backs of the armed forces in hostile climes and of polar explorers for whom nothing but the best would do. The shooting man being a little set in his ways was slower to wake up to its possibilities; but Ventile has now won a secure niche in the sporting outfitter's window.

Various firms made up shooting coats from the Ventile fabric, typically the Applejac shooting jacket made by Carol Cocks in Carlisle. Well cut and smart, as well as comfortable and practical, it seems to have solved many of the problems associated with wax. There are roomy pockets, a stud-on hood, and removable quilted lining; cuffs and pocket edges are reinforced with leather trim for hard wear and appearance. This coat has withstood rigorous testing in the heaviest of rainstorms, and not only kept the wearer bone dry but remained soft to the touch. The sleeves are generously cut to allow freedom of arm movement.

Ventile is made up by Country Sports, Thane Slioch, Hilltrek, Rascher of Germany and L'Esquimau. Retail outlets include Farlows of Pall Mall, John Norris, Purdey, William Powell and Lanes of Coventry.

A variation on the theme, in a similar cloth and with the same properties as Ventile, is Suplesse from Thomas Mason. Made up by Kate Gill of South Devon, it is a two-in-one jacket with sleeves and a back section which may be

One of the breed of new 'breathing' fabrics, a wonderful new coat from
Applejac which combines comfort, style and rugged, hard weather resistance.
Comfort in the field is all-important if you are to enjoy the day

This shooting suit from Norton, the Saville Row tailors, in conjunction with
Boss, represents the Rolls Royce of shooting clothing. Lined with breathing
Gore-Tex and made throughout of hand-crafted tweed, this outfit is for the
shooter who has everything and is prepared to pay extra for the best

removed on a hot day, thus transforming the coat into a waistcoat, the spare section being carried by means of a patent strap device. This idea is a novel way of dealing with those shooting days when hard walking is interspersed with spells of standing still, and when the weather might vary wildly in temperature. Both coats comprise a modern and smart way to dress on a formal day.

The Gill Pins country coat combines softness and 'breathability' with uncompromising rain-defeating properties. As an added refinement the sleeves and shoulder portion can be removed quickly in warm conditions and easily replaced, making this a coat for all seasons

There is still the option of the full tweed or Loden shooting suit in two- or three-piece; this was popular in the Edwardian era and had a style all its own. Good, heavy tweed is all but waterproof, and will absorb gallons of rain while continuing to keep the body warm and ventilated. I had a suit of this style made by Hebden Cord at Hebden Bridge in Yorkshire, where they know a thing or two about rain and making tweeds to keep it out. A suit like that will last more than a lifetime and speaks of all the tradition of the shooting field.

It is possible to improve upon even that delight if you add Gore-Tex to the mixture. This is the breathing material *par excellence*, not cloth at all, but a stuff very like fine polythene known to science as 'polytetrafluoroethylene' (PTFE). The Gore-Tex membrane has nine billion pores per square inch, each one smaller than a droplet of water but larger than a molecule of water vapour, so that sweat can vent out while rainwater is kept at bay. Like Ventile, Gore-Tex is used widely by the armed forces for foul weather gear, and also by mountaineers. Clothing incorporating Gore-Tex is made by, amongst others, L'Esquimaux, Hallett Thornton, Herbert Johnson, John Partridge, Kede, Musto and the Remington line from Hull Cartridge Company.

PTFE is incorporated as an inner membrane in the coat; you would not tell by looking that it was there, for the garment is, to all intents and purposes, a normal tweed shooting jacket—only when the going gets hard or the weather foul does the hidden magic start to work. Initially the trouble experienced with the prototype Gore-Tex was not the material, but the fact that the manufacturers of the clothing *sewed* it in, giving it a neat row of holes at every joint. Testers reported that it leaked, and of course it did, as it had received myriad punctures. That problem has been overcome. My first shooting coat of that type was a Chrysalis: I have it still and find it excellent in every way.

Take Gore-Tex and hand it to a Saville Row tailor of the likes of, for example, Walter Norton and Son, and you end up with the Rolls Royce of jackets, a coat to rival the sun, moon and stars together. Clobber like that seems too good to be exposed to mud and brambles in places where rain is liable to lash down. Fear not, for this garment is of superb quality tweed with a quilted lining for extra warmth, and the all-important Gore-Tex sandwiched in between. The wearer is warm but never hot, cool but never cold, and at no time damp, no matter how hard it rains or how many miles he has slogged over a red-hot grouse moor. The best tailoring in the world sees to it that some fifty hours are devoted to one coat, with the result that it has a bounce, a 'feel' and a cut which alone bestow the sensation of well-being in the wearer, and that the shades are the muted, subtle tints of the countryside, of bracken, old stubble and heather; all promote a feeling of pride. Your clothing becomes more than just inanimate kit, it is part of your personality, an old and valued friend. Such things may be small enough, but every little helps to promote your enjoyment of your shooting day and helps you shoot that little bit better as you are confident that your equipment will not let you down.

The coat is the most expensive piece of clothing you will buy, from the waxproof at the least costly end, the Ventile type next, and the Gore-Tex/ tweed from a London tailor at the top end which is by no means cheap. The choice depends on how much shooting you intend to do and the depth of your pocket; but in my experience, the British sportsman has tended never to stint himself on his accoutrements and clobber.

Final Tips

So much for the basic equipment which, in some form or other, the game Shot will be expected to acquire. For the young Shot, compromise is certainly acceptable as only the over-indulged buys the whole lot in one go. Most of us collect it a piece at a time and gradually improve upon it as funds increase and more prestigious invitations accrue. The beginner ought to try and get a pair of plus-twos, but the rest of his clothing may be improvised as long as it obeys the simple rules of being tidy, unobtrusive and, in his own interests, weatherproof.

A final tip is to have a checklist near the door by which you leave to go shooting: run your eye down it as you are about to depart to make sure you have left nothing behind. It is very easy to leave a vital item at home—we have all done it, and all it takes is, say, your lunch, dog lead, dog whistle or Wellingtons to be at home when you are elsewhere and in need of them, for a potentially super day to be ruined. The Game Conservancy has made a list in the form of a plastic label which you can attach to, say, guncase or cartridge bag. I prefer to make my own and I urge the reader to do the same; the list is then suited to yourself. You might, for example, be taking medication for some small but troublesome ailment and it would not do to leave the pills at home. My own list reads as follows:

Gun
Slip, motor-case, pull-through, cleaning rags
Cartridges
Cartridge bag, spare cartons
Whistles (dog and Acme Thunderer)
Dog
Dog lead, towel, handful of dog biscuits
Wallet and cash; (suitable denomination for tip)
Shooting stick
Spectacles
Food
Coat, hat, Wellies, shoes for indoors
Mittens
Sticking plasters

This list is personal to me, but to leave any one of those things at home would spoil a day, and in the rush of an early start it is all too easy to do so unless you spare the two minutes it takes to run a spot-check. You get into the habit of not leaving home without running your eye down it. You might not need everything on it (shooting stick, for example) but at least you leave it behind on purpose.

5
Safety in the Field

A shotgun of any bore is a fearsome weapon; in the hands of the dangerous, greedy, careless or inexperienced at close range it can be deadly, and at longer range even a single pellet can blind or maim. Every year there is a sorry catalogue of shooting accidents, yet most of these are avoidable—the rules to prevent them are few and simple. On the whole more accidents occur on the rough shoot where only two or three are gathered together, or sometimes just one person on his own; very often a consequence of the lack of structure which is part of the rough shoot's very attraction. There are times when you are uncertain of where other people are, chances come at unexpected angles and from any direction, dogs are working tight cover, and the whole situation is potentially volatile. The rough shooter needs very strict gun discipline.

The driven shoot being a more formal and orchestrated occasion, tends to suffer to a lesser degree. The direction from which game approaches is predictable, although not its height nor its angle of approach. Also clear signals are given, before and after which it is not permissible to shoot; and those in the driven field tend to be more experienced Guns, although this is no guarantee of how safe they are. On the driven shoot there is less need for Guns to struggle through cover in a potentially dangerous fashion, to scramble over barbed wire or negotiate muddy streams, all of which are part and parcel of the rough shooter's sporting life.

However, accidents do occur, and while it is impossible to eradicate them entirely—in the same way that there are no absolute standards of security—they may be reduced to a minimum by a strict observance of the rules. The famous poem by Mark Beaufoy, addressed to his son when he started shooting, appears at the end of this chapter (p93), and I make no excuse for parading it yet again for safety is such an important thing that it is impossible to make too much of it. To shoot with those who take chances with your own life each time you are in their company is not to enjoy your sport, and it is cold comfort to your widow to be told that you were the victim of a criminally dangerous fellow sportsman.

The first, last and only rule which umbrellas all others is that at no time and under no circumstances should a gun be pointed in any direction where, if it went off, it would endanger the life or limb of yourself or anyone else. In fact as soon as we make that rule we must begin to compromise, though without at any time losing sight of the original tablet of stone upon which it is engraved. For example, a gun may be carried muzzles upmost and thus apparently in perfect safety in a waggon on the way to the next drive—but, were it to be left inadvertently loaded and were it to go off, the pellets might bounce off the roof of the vehicle and cause damage. A gun aimed at even quite a high pheasant has been known to spray one or more pellets in unexpected directions due to ricochets off the tight feathers, and this is even more of a risk with wildfowl.

A gun carried in a gunslip is often pointed in all sorts of frightening directions, for the owner seems to believe that the slip removes the need for the rules he would impose on himself were the gun uncovered. But a cartridge left in the breech, a sudden jar or a drop, and more than just another myth explodes.

When walking from drive to drive the gun should be in the slip, and the slip zipped shut and carried on the shoulder by its strap. The other way is for the gun to be carried broken over the user's arm, as is the absolute rule on any clay shooting ground—where the standards of safety are uncompromisingly high. There has been correspondence in the sporting press about the wisdom or otherwise of carrying a gun thus. Warnings of strain to the hinge pin, of the risk of foreign bodies or rain, snow or mud entering the action, and the belief that the gun was not designed to be carried in such a way. There may just be the vestige of half a point in this, but the balance comes down heavily in favour of the 'gun broken' rule; everyone can see it is unloaded and of not the slightest risk to anyone—which is more than you can say of a gun in a slip carried any old how.

A gun may be carried military fashion over the shoulder, but only with the trigger-guard uppermost so that the muzzles never waver from pointing skywards. This is all very well, but the arm aches after a while and there is a risk that you forget and allow the gun to roll round so that the barrels are aiming at the Adam's apple of anyone unfortunate enough to be walking behind you.

When you arrive at your peg, remove the gun from the slip and break it; on the signal to start the drive you may load. It is a good habit to close the breech of a shotgun by moving the stock up to the barrels and not vice versa; to bring the barrels to the stock brings dogs, human legs and other hazardous objects into the line of fire. Stock to muzzle, and the barrels remain pointing safely at the ground.

Standing at your peg you should be alert and ready for a quick and unexpected shot and your gun should be held accordingly. The general rule is that the fewer and shorter the movements required to bring the gun to bear on the target the better, especially when you get older and a little less nimble. Do not gaze round (apart from the necessary check to ascertain the position of the picker-up), or stare at the clouds, roll cigarettes, light pipes, unwrap sweets or wander over to the chap next door and start an animated conversation. One of the best Shots in England attributes his sucess and uncanny good fortune to the fact that he concentrates totally when at his peg so that when a bird approaches he is never caught napping. That one-second advantage over a less alert neighbour always gave him an edge.

The gun may be held at the ready, muzzles up, right hand on the grip and fore-finger laid along the trigger-guard, never clenched round the trigger itself. The muzzles should be as close as possible to where you expect a bird to appear so your movements will be minimal when that moment arrives. It is acceptable to hold the gun with the stock resting on your hip with the muzzles almost vertical or angled slightly forwards. From this position it is also easy to mount quickly and bring the barrels to bear. Some adopt a more casual approach and hold the gun trigger-guard up over the shoulder in the military style I have mentioned for use when walking. This is acceptable if you are expecting no shot for some time or just to give the other muscles a rest, but in the event of a surprise woodcock, you have left yourself an awful lot to do before the gun is on target.

When a bird approaches, you make an instant assessment as to whether it is to be yours or that of a neighbour; and in the case of the former, whether or not it will be safe to fire at it. A bird which flies halfway between you would be left by purists, but I see nothing wrong in a neighbour calling loudly 'Yours!' so that you have clear precedence—or if you are quick you will call the invitation first. A second bird following the same path is the prerogative of the other Gun, and so on. Beaufoy said '. . . better spared, is a pheasant than one shared'; true enough, but with a bit of give and take and some quick thinking, this problem need not arise.

Shooting down the line is one of the greatest and most commonly committed crimes, often carried out by those who should know better. The rule is not to shoot a bird, or even point your gun, over the head of another person. Thus when a bird approaches from in front where for various reasons it cannot be shot, you must on no account allow your muzzles to track it on and over the head of a neighbour, whether or not you fire. The correct procedure is to pick up the bird as it is approaching, realise in good time that it would be better taken behind, dismount the gun, turn round, and remount to take it after it has passed by. In this way at no time is your gun pointing anywhere near anyone else in the shooting field.

Another source of danger is the low bird, wherever it might appear. Not only is a low bird often easy to shoot and therefore unsporting, it creates all sorts of risks to the rest of the field. The low, close bird is either missed clean due to an undeveloped pattern, or is blown to bits for the same reason—and what sportsman can derive any satisfaction from that? Fire at a bird low in front and you risk shot cutting through the bushes and injuring beaters, dogs or other Guns. Fire at a low one behind (bound to be a runner even if you get it, and hence unsatisfactory), and the picker-up hidden from view runs the same risk. There is no reason why such a bird should be fired at or even addressed; it is widely held that only greedy or selfish Shots with no care for the safety of others take such chances, and who wants to be tarred with that particular brush?

Woodcock are a law unto themselves. Everyone likes to shoot a woodcock, for it is a great prize on a shooting day. There are some estates where they are protected. The woodcock has probably caused more normally sane and safe Shots to behave dangerously than anything else. That mothy, flickering flight with its sudden changes of direction, lazily dodging through the tree trunks, the excited cries 'Cock Up!', and that strange aura surrounding the bird, all weave a spell which makes men mad. One moment the 'cock is in open sky and perfectly safe to shoot, the next it is down to ground level or in front of bushes where a stop might well be hiding. Not for nothing did one old keeper attribute his longevity to the fact that every time he heard the cry 'Woodcock!' he flung himself face down in the bracken.

There is no answer, and nobody can proffer definitive advice on how to counter woodcock magic. Try your best to stick to the time-honoured rules, and take the bird when it is safe—but hold your gun high and safely when it becomes an uncertain target. The hardest thing to do is to dismount your gun from a woodcock, but to do so denotes a shooter of real self-discipline and control, totally unselfish and utterly safety-conscious. Sadly there are few of us left!

Ground game too calls for special care. On many shoots the rule is that *no*

The game cart man is a key person on any shoot

Left: A beating team has its own camaraderie

Top: The keeper feeds his birds in high
summer; they are the promise of sport to come

Above: Game will stay if the habitat
is welcoming

Snap shooting in a ride

ground game *at all* may be shot, as hard experience has proved that this practice is potentially dangerous in a crowded shooting field. The shot whizzes not up into the empty air, but onto the ground where flints cause ricochets, and human legs 'lurk behind the leafy screen'. Quite often a dog might be hot on the tail of the rabbit or hare but just concealed in the cover, behind the hedge, or down and out of sight in the ditch, and so many have been inadvertently shot as they popped out. The case need not be laboured. To shoot a dog on a shooting day is a dreadful experience for all, especially the shooter and the owner of the dog, and for the sake of a rabbit it seems hardly worth the risk. Even on shoots where ground game may be shot, take the utmost care: it is my advice that when a chance occurs, you should suffer from a sudden bout of diplomatic blindness. Much the same is true should you be invited to shoot foxes. A fox is another man's sport, and anyway, shooting them is no job for a formal day but should be left to the keeper. The blind spot should strike again when old Reynard comes loping through.

At the end of the drive, put your gun in its slip and carry it as before to where you are needed next. In the shoot vehicle, which might be a trailer or covered waggon, sit with your gun stock on the ground between your feet the barrels pointing upwards. When you get on and off the trailer, pass the gun to someone waiting below and do the same when you clamber in if uncertain of your footing. Thoughtful hosts will usually provide a ladder, steps, or at worst a straw bale to help you up, but it takes only a second to pass your gun, and this is a far better practice than to risk a stumble and have your cherished weapon crash to the ground with disastrous results.

It is slightly inconsistent that a gun in a slip may be passed in what might otherwise constitute a dangerous manner, the slip bestowing the illusion of safety. For when the gun is uncovered, more stringent rules apply. To hand a shotgun to someone else it should be broken, shown to be unloaded, and handed over stock first. Pass the gun unbroken and the receiver himself will instantly break it to ensure it is empty. When you pick up a gun or take it from a cupboard, check automatically that it is empty; the action becomes second nature. Many years ago I returned home after shooting, took my gun from its slip, broke it and found two unfired cartridges in the chambers. I went hot and cold in an instant; how on earth could they have remained there after all the checks of which I was so proud? I would have sworn the gun was safe, but I would have been wrong. I have not made that mistake since, but it *could* have ended in fearful tragedy; I tell the tale to indicate that no-one is infallible.

When you cross a tricky obstacle such as a narrow bridge or a ditch or scramble through a hedge, the gun should be broken and the cartridges removed. On the driven shoot you will not often be called upon to negotiate difficult country—such is one of the delights of rough shooting—but it does happen. A shotgun with the safety catch on 'Safe' is anything but. The mainsprings are still under full compression, and all that the 'safe' means is that there is a sliver of metal which prevents the trigger being pulled. No mechanical device is 100 per cent reliable, and when a gun which is old or worn is dropped or even dealt a smart blow, a hammer could easily fall and detonate the cartridge.

A stumble or slip might be enough to cause an accident, and the breaking of the simple rule with which we started. If you *do* happen to stumble or fall, check the gun carefully for damage such as a dent in the barrels, which is not only extremely costly but also very dangerous if the gun is fired again. This leads to another good habit which is to glance down your barrels from time to time before loading. The slightest obstruction, the veriest wisp of mud or snow will cause a burst, the consequences of which can be disastrous. It happens occasionally that through some remarkable fluke a faulty cartridge leaves an obstruction such as a wad stuck in the barrels. So every time there is an uncharacteristic noise or recoil from the cartridge, it pays to check the barrels.

A friend shooting at a friendly clay shoot fired two cartridges at two clays and missed them both. One of the shots sounded a little odd. My friend broke the gun and ejected his two cases, but one of them I saw from the corner of my eye comprised the brass head of the case only and not the plastic cyclinder. Thinking I had probably mis-seen it, I hunted in the grass all the same, more from idle curiosity than anything. There, sure enough, deep in the grass, was the brass head of a cartridge case. In the meantime Andrew had reloaded and was on the point of calling 'Pull!' for his next pair.

Something made me say, 'Hang on a minute Andrew; just check your barrels'. He unloaded, looked down—and sure enough, the whole of the plastic cylinder was jammed in the barrel a few inches forward of the chamber. Had he fired again, the barrel would certainly have burst and done who can guess what damage?

Ricochets are an underrated source of danger. I had an experience of one when a youngster, when I had been invited to an end-of-season cock shoot on the estate of the squire, a rare privilege and an occasion to be relished. One drive was through a small, round wood in the middle of the park, a wood surrounded by those iron railings favoured in Edwardian times. Ground game was the rule and I fired in all safety at a rabbit passing at the foot of the fence. However, the old squire, who was himself shooting on my right, gave a strangled grunt and began capering about clutching his neck, whence blood trickled. He was almost at my side, but a single pellet had struck the angle of the supporting post and come back at nearly 90° and stuck in his neck. It was a bad moment, but he took it sportingly enough and my invitations did not, as I was certain they would, dry up immediately. Who would have considered that a dangerous shot, in spite of the outcome?

Pellets can behave in the strangest and most unpredictable ways. As well as 'fliers', or pellets on the outside of the pattern which whizz off at 45° of the muzzle, pellets striking water at any but the acutest angle will zip onwards on a new trajectory with their velocity undiminished. There is a great risk involved in shooting wounded duck down on the water, and on many sensible shoots it is strictly forbidden to do so.

Water was the cause of trouble for another friend who sent his dog for a running hen pheasant. The dog was gone for a long time and my friend worked his way through the little belt to the stream beyond. There, halfway across the river, was the hen pheasant swimming to freedom as only a pheasant can. In an instant he raised his gun and shot the bird—but it was not the pheasant: it was the head of his beloved dog. Mercifully it survived five pellets in its skull. There is no such thing as absolute safety in anything in which human beings are involved.

Dogs can cause trouble in other ways. Never and on no account tether your dog to your belt when you are shooting. This is asking for trouble, for the moment you raise your gun to fire the unruly beast will probably rush off in anticipation of a retrieve, heaving you off balance, sending your first shot heaven knows where and your second straight at the approaching head keeper. If you insist on taking an unsteady dog, take one of those giant corkscrews as well so you can screw it to the ground a safe distance from you; or employ someone to keep it on the lead. Dogs have caused many shooting accidents one way or another.

When you reach your peg, make sure you have a firm and level place on which to stand. Ploughed land or a muddy slope make for uncertain grip and stance, and since all good shooting starts from the feet, a slip could prove dangerous. It is wise to stamp down a little level platform when first you arrive at an uneven spot.

Before you fire, be absolutely certain what it is you are aiming at. Human legs have been mistaken for rabbits, protected birds have been shot in error, dogs have been accidentally peppered (and worse), and all sorts of mishaps have occurred due to the shooter being too hasty. Some years ago our shooting field had in the beating line a small West Highland terrier. It was a wonderful flushing dog, and could be relied on to move every pheasant from a field of sugarbeet. You rarely saw the dog, it simply bustled about under the canopy of leaves doing its job.

The beaters came down the sugarbeet and up went the cry of 'Fox! Fox!'. On our shoot Reynard is not spared as we are wild bird country and the hunt never comes within miles. This fox had been plaguing us for some time and it seemed that at long last we had got him cornered. Every Gun waited eagerly; who would be the one to claim the scalp? The fox slipped down the side of the beet coming my way; at extreme range he nipped back under the leaves, and I presumed continued to come forward. At the very spot I expected him to appear he popped out his head; the gun was on it in an instant, the safety off, my finger applying pressure on the trigger when some sixth sense made me pause.

You have guessed it: I was looking down the barrels at the West Highlander, covered in brown mud, just stopping for a breather and peeping out to see where he had got to. That was the luckiest dog alive, for all of us had seen the fox and were eager to bag it, and we all expected to see it with *such certainty* that whatever popped out its head we were sure would be Charlie. Never allow excitement to cloud your judgement but keep a cool head.

It might be that having taken all steps yourself to make sure *you* are behaving safely, you witness unsafe conduct in another. This is a hard one if you are a novice or a newcomer, in which case your best bet is to have a quiet word with your host or the shoot captain who will do what is needed. Otherwise you have no choice but to grasp the nettle yourself. Fail to speak up, and *you* might be the unhappy victim of a criminally dangerous shot, cold comfort to you as you lie in the ambulance or when your widow comes to collect your stuff. Even if you care nothing about your own safety, then what about the next person to come within range of those carelessly wafted barrels?

Speak up: a true sportsman won't mind—on the contrary, he will thank you for pointing out his mistake. Walking the moor one day I glanced down to the next Gun who was well below me on the hill: I could see right down his gun barrels, and he is the safest of Shots. Politely but quite firmly I told him that I could see what size shot he was using—and he was visibly shaken, immediately apologetic, and thanked me for drawing it to his attention. Incident closed!

If the danger persists, take evasive action; it will spoil your day, but better that than end up full of shot. Steer clear of that man and that place thereafter. If he is that bad it is surprising that others haven't commented upon it before, but in the shooting field you will see some conduct which would make your hair curl, and it seems to pass unrebuked.

Be careful if you are shooting near livestock: sheep on a grouse moor can be a nuisance, although on lowground shoots it is likely that you will be kept away from cattle or horses. Shooting this very season a shot was fired by a Gun who was unaware that a lady on a horse accompanied by two youngsters on ponies were approaching from behind the hedge. At the shot one pony reared and the child fell off, fortunately with no damage apart from a scare. It was not the fault of the shooter, nor of the riders who did not know that shooting was going on; but it serves as a warning to be aware of any animals, especially horses being ridden.

The BASC have coined the expression: 'Safety is a level of consciousness, not a fortunate series of events'. I add that it all boils down to a mixture of common courtesy and good sense.

If you are to earn a reputation in the formal shooting field, let it be that of a generous, unselfish, sporting and above all a safe Shot. Anyone with a few lessons and a pinch of experience can learn to hit a fair proportion of what he fires at, so there is little mileage in being the best Shot in England; better be the safest, and invitations will come thick and fast. Nobody likes you to be too clever, and surely the most unpopular man in the English shooting field is he who never misses.

Standards tend to be high and fools are not suffered gladly; in the UK we suffer fewer gun accidents than anywhere else in Europe where the sport is followed, a tribute to the care and the traditions of safety which we have built up and passed on from generation to generation.

Until the newcomer has mastered the simple rules of field safety, and developed the self-discipline to curb his natural excitement and competitiveness, there is little point in his joining a shoot or even accepting an invitation.

A Father's Advice to his Son

If a sportsman true you'd be,
listen carefully to me

Never, never let your gun
pointed be at anyone;
that it may unloaded be
matters not the least to me.

When a hedge or fence you cross,
though of time it cause a loss,
from your gun the cartridge take,
for the greater safety's sake.

If 'twixt you and neighbouring gun
birds may fly or beasts may run,
let this maxim e'er be thine:
FOLLOW NOT ACROSS THE LINE.

Stops and beaters oft unseen
lurk behind some leafy screen;
calm and steady always be:
NEVER SHOOT WHERE YOU CAN'T SEE.

Keep your place and silent be:
game can hear and game can see;
don't be greedy, better spared
is a pheasant than one shared.

You may kill or you may miss,
but at all times think of this:
all the pheasants ever bred
won't repay for one man dead.

Commander Mark Beaufoy

6
Straight Shooting
by Michael W. Alldis

Probably more has been written in British books on shooting skills with regard to the driven bird, than any other subject. The classic British shot is the driven bird. Ten times more pheasant, partridge or grouse are shot by driving than by walking up, and the driven shoot is firmly British based. The continent has copied us, especially Spain for driven partridge, whilst the New World still walks them up or shoots over pointing dogs. Yet many Americans travel here for this uniquely British experience, and by early August the shooting schools are working flat out re-teaching the citizens of Florida to North Dakota to blot the bird out and keep the gun moving after firing the shot. Then it's off to the moors for the grouse. Some come back in November for a little high tower coaching for the pheasant, but not as many, the Americans preferring wild game to the driven bird.

Physical Fitness

Shooting driven game requires reasonable physical fitness, good co-ordination and eyesight strong enough to pass the driving test. One of my clients who arrived in a £40,000 Porsche was unable to read line 3 of an eyesight card—line 7 is normal vision for the driving test. He returned two weeks later, with glasses, and has shot consistently well ever since. The moral of the story, have your eyes tested frequently for good shooting and safe driving.

A well fitted gun is important, particularly to those past the middle years. So often the gun so painstakingly measured by Percy Stanbury or Norman Clark thirty years ago, is now mounted by a shooter who has gained two stone in weight, having stopped smoking at fifty odd, whose jowls have dropped (not only the ladies need a face-lift) and whose shoulders have rounded and stooped. A re-measure every ten years after the age of forty is money well spent, and always after permanent weight loss or gain.

Master Eye

Master eye is important if you shoot with both eyes open. Many people shoot perfectly well with the non-gun-side eye closed, and many have ruined their shooting by listening to friends who say 'keep both eyes open'. As a general rule of thumb, if you want to close an eye, do so, after you have checked with a qualified coach that you need to. Modern living, and in particular computer screens (VDUs) play tricks with master eyes and can alter them temporarily, and sometimes permanently. A client of mine, a potato futures dealer, shot very well with his Purdey; an hour's wash and brush-up was all he needed every year, and that was more of a confidence booster than any re-teaching exercise. And then his master eye altered from right to left. In fact the cure was easy; all you need to do is close the eye just before swinging through the bird, and all should be well again. Why the change? Where before he had traded with a pocket book, he now traded from a screen: in a period of three months the effect of this was to alter his master eye.

The moral: be aware of the problem, and check your master eye by pointing with the index finger of the hand you hold the barrels with, at an object with both eyes open. Close each eye in turn, and when the finger appears to move this is your master eye; it should be on the same side as the shoulder on which you mount the gun. Another good test is to make a hole the size of a pound coin in the centre of an A4 sheet. Holding the paper with both hands held straight in front of you, and with both eyes open, look through the hole at an object. Concentrating on this object, draw the paper towards your face. The eye which is looking through the hole when the paper reaches your nose is your master eye. If your master eye is not your gun-side eye, you must see a qualified coach.

We should by now have a shooter whose eyes are visually acceptable, who is fit in wind and limb, with a gun of today's fit and not of twenty years ago, and who is shooting off the correct shoulder, hopefully two-eyed, but if not, one-eyed will do 95 per cent as well. You will note I have not mentioned cross-over or dog-leg stocks for master eye problems. They have their place when physical problems occur with a shooter, but they are the last resort, being ungainly, bad for recoil, expensive and hard to sell. Avoid them if you can. They were very much favoured between the wars, because of the part-amputees after the Kaiser's war. Just of late, due to sloppy orthopaedic surgery and physiotherapy following motor accidents, a number of clients have been unable to turn their front arm enough to grip the fore-end. Though I hate the look, we have made a 'Tommy gun' fore-end, which works well. I even like the feel of the grip myself, and reckon I shoot better with it. Of course, it'll never catch on—but then they said that about over-and-unders, didn't they!

Shooting Technique

The driven game shooter has four main shots: the direct approaching shot, that to the left, to the right and behind. In the following paragraphs the reader should understand that I am writing for right-handed Shots, who in fact make up 85 per cent of the shooting population.

Weight Distribution and Stance

All good shooting starts from the feet and what they stand on. Always clear a small 'ballroom area' prior to shooting in rough ground—if the keeper is any good he'll have done it for you, and you should tip accordingly. I have always admired the many diagrams of foot movement in certain older books on shooting. My mother was a qualified dancing teacher, and on seeing these in the late 50's she remarked that they looked like a chart for the fox-trot issued by the Imperial Institute of Teachers of Dance. Seriously, all you need to know is, point your front foot where you expect to shoot the bird—though most of you will forget this completely in the heat of the moment. Video cameras are now common on many shoots, and on all the ones that I have seen in the last ten years, not one Gun in fifty seems to move his feet to the bird; and many of these were in fact my own clients who had demonstrated brilliant ballet steps at the clays. Finally, don't spread the feet too much; 9in between the heels is enough: too wide apart inhibits lateral swing and makes you look like a lady of the night in the business position.

Weight distribution is important. Shoot off the front foot like Stanbury or the back foot like Churchill; like closing the eye, this is mostly up to you. If you are thin, like Percy, the front foot is for you; if portly, like Robert (and me) then use the back foot. The older you get the more you will favour the back foot because your back gets stiffer.

Holding the Gun

Avoid the long front arm—it doesn't help when you mount the gun and may well cause you to lift the head, and therefore to shoot high. Lateral movement is also inhibited. It looks pretty and became common for a time as everybody aped royal exponents, starting with Edward the Seventh. However, if the truth were known, they would have shot better with their hand further back along the fore-end. But then, it's difficult to tell the monarch to move his hands if he doesn't want to, as Mrs Simpson found.

The Approaching Shot

The directly approaching shot is the easiest. Mount the gun from behind the bird, firmly to the face and shoulder, blot the bird out with the gun barrels, pull the trigger, and—you hope—watch the bird drop in front of you. Sounds easy, and it is. The main reasons for missing are 1) not wishing to lose sight of the bird; 2) lifting the head; and 3) mounting the gun too early on a bird seen from far away. The cures are as follows: 1) say to yourself, if I can see it I will miss it; 2) feel the pressure of the stock, and until you do, don't fire; and 3) after seeing the bird, look down and count to three (five if you dare), look up and then shoot.

Right-to-Left Shot (to the left)

Either swing from behind the bird at a rate dictated by speed and distance, and fire at the moment of passing and keep swinging. Or, if you prefer to see some lead, mount on the bird, point at it, make the appropriate gap for speed and distance, fire and keep moving. Both methods work well, and you must decide which you prefer. *Do not attempt maintained lead for game: it* works well for skeet, and not much else. The main reason for missing, except incorrect lead, is shooting too high: the cure is to sweep by the belly of the bird.

Left-to-Right Shot (to the right)

This is more difficult than the other way as the gun moving away from the body inhibits swing. The methods of shooting are the same as for right to lefts. The reasons for missing are 1) lack of lead caused by inhibited movement; and 2) shooting low because of the shoulder dropping as you turn. The cures are 1) say to yourself, I must swing faster on my right, or I must see more lead on my right; and 2) bring the right leg forward to stop the shoulder dropping. This has disadvantages, however, as you will probably forget, or if you do remember, will find that swing is further inhibited. Better is to say to yourself, I must sweep over the back of the bird. In other words, shoot high to the right.

Shooting Behind, etc

The behind shot is required more for grouse and partridge than pheasant. Here you *must* move your feet if you are to stand any chance. Pivot on the back foot, gun up as you pass through the line. Try not to rush, and shoot slightly under the bird. The most common fault is missing above, especially

at grouse. However, I have had one particular case where the shooter knew he had to be slightly below, but after missing a few went lower still; the rot set in, and he rarely bothered to fire behind—by the time he got to me he was missing them 3ft below. All was well in two shots, but it was an unexpected fault from a highly experienced Shot and a senior member of the gun trade. The best cure for shooting above is to say 'take your time', and shoot the belly of the bird; the pattern will take care of any drop.

Birds in a Pack

By now you will be saying, 'All very well old chap, but when they're thick and fast I will forget all you have told me'. You won't if you remember that even in the biggest flush you can only shoot birds one at a time. If you rush you will miss, if you slow down you will kill. Taking a half-second longer per bird only means that you will shoot two or three less in a minute. All the very top game Shots look as if they never hurry, and they don't, but they kill more than most, with very high kills-to-cartridge ratios. For the last two years I have kept meticulous records of my own game shooting. In 1989/90, for my 442 birds I shot 733 cartridges, averaging 1.658 cartridges per bird. I seriously hurt my hand on the last day of 1989, and up until then the average was about 1.5.

In 1990/91, for my 492 birds, I shot 748 cartridges, an average of 1.520 cartridges per bird. I know this proves nothing, other than a generally

higher-than-average kills-to-cartridge ratio, but this is achieved by a deep resolve not to be rushed. I will not be repeating the exercise this season, or probably ever again as it requires considerable effort to count cartridges, etc. I also suspect that if one went further it might lead to picking easy birds to beat the averages.

The High Bird

The other bird that so worries a Gun is that very high bird all on its own, the one you wish would fly over your neighbour so he can make a fool of himself. Generally, you will miss this bird behind. So say to yourself, I must miss it so far in front it's silly, I must have the confidence to go too far. You won't, your brain won't let you, and you will succeed. If by pure chance you miss in front, and only one Gun in ten does, there is no shame—the rest of the party is probably only too relieved it was not their turn to make a public Horlicks.

Left-and-Rights, Under-and-Overs . . .

Left-and-rights, right-and-lefts, under-and-overs, over-and-unders: all are terms to indicate two birds being shot by the same gun rapidly, and without reloading. How long is 'rapidly'? This is a difficult question! I have always felt that the first bird should still be dead in the air while the second one is shot, though with low grouse this may not be possible. To shoot left-and-rights well, you must be able to work out which is to be your second bird while shooting the first. Decoyed pigeon shooting can help with this. Will Garfit, who is a *Shooting Times* 1st Eleven Shot, says his pigeon shooting has helped him tremendously in assessing the second bird and where to kill it. However, I have a cautionary tale: in 1988 I shot a highish hen bird well in front, and then moved on to a similar cock which I also killed. A split-second later the gun was knocked from my hands by the deceased hen and fell some five feet in front of me. No damage was done, but the possibility of the hen striking the gun *before* the second barrel was discharged does not bear thinking about. I was accompanied by two ladies, neither of whom saw the hen because like me, they were concentrating on the cock. Motto: beware falling birds (both types). Perhaps the most important thing one can say to any game shooter, other than concerning safety which we will come to in a moment, is shoot confidently, expect to kill your bird—and you will. Be diffident, and you won't. Once you think you've killed it, pull the trigger, and don't try to make it a better shot—you won't, you will miss. Confidence is all.

Safety

Safety is the most important aspect of driven game shooting and so merits in-depth discussion.

1) Your gun will only be loaded during drives, and then only between the signal to start the drive and to finish it. This will usually be a whistle or a horn.

2) At all other times the gun will be carried either in a slip, barrel end downwards, or over the arm in the broken position.

3) You will only have with you cartridges suitable for the day or your gun, eg if a 12-bore gun, you must not have 20-bore cartridges with you. It is unwise to have heavy loads, eg 3s, as these will wholly destroy any birds that you shoot at game-shooting ranges.

4) You will check before shooting that your barrels have no obstructions. If using a pair, check both guns.

5) When at the stand, you will check before shooting where your neighbours are, the direction of the beaters, any stops and in particular pickers-up. In many cases, when pickers-up are accidentally shot it is largely their own fault because they come too close to the guns; their proper position is at least 300 yards back, well out of shot, to deal with runners. A polite word with the organiser can usually rectify this unsafe practice.

6) Never, ever, swing through the line. Always raise your gun if you are forced to shoot behind. A safety margin of 90° in front and the same behind should be adhered to. In a grouse butt it is advisable to mark this with your cartridge bag and gun slip, if stop poles are not provided.

7) The vertical angle of permitted fire should not be less than 45° in flat country, and a great deal more where hills put the beaters above you. Obviously, for grouse, the verticals do not apply, and the keeper will blow a horn to indicate no shooting in front, when the beaters close to 300 yards.

8) At the end of the day, clean your gun and check for any damage. Even if your loader has done this for you, check yourself—it will be *your* hands it blows up in.

9) You may be a walking Gun behind the beaters, in which case your job is to shoot only birds going back. You should check if a picker-up is trailing you. Walking with a loaded gun doubles the risk, and great care should be taken in ensuring a safe foothold when shooting. I have only hurt myself once when game shooting and this was when walking. I turned quickly in heavy plough and managed to twist a knee so badly that I couldn't go to work for a week. Whilst on the subject of walking, though you will be empty between drives, great care should be taken when crossing ditches, fences, hedges, walls and suchlike: the gun is best passed to another while you clear the obstacle, and returned to you when you have completed the manoeuvre.

10) Lastly, never fire where you can't see. So often people lurk where you don't expect, and very often they are not even shoot servants, but members of the public who have no business to be where they are.

Ground game and woodcock, snipe and duck are species that appear on driven days. My advice on ground game is, don't bother, even if they are on the menu. Many shoots sensibly forbid them altogether. Shooting low is always dangerous and you can't get lower than on the ground. Woodcock should be treated with great care, they fly low and jink and turn, often in dense cover. If in doubt, don't. The same is true to a lesser extent with snipe, though they tend not to appear in woodland, which makes them safer. Driven duck can be appallingly low and I would hope no-one would shoot these for ethical reasons, let alone safety. Duck are always higher than you think, so always give them just a little more lead than your brain wants to let you.

Double Guns and a Loader

Most people using double guns probably don't need to, but a pair has a certain cachet, and it certainly provides a spare gun for a breakdown. Having said that, in 33 years of driven game shooting I have only once had a gun breakdown. In fact most driven game shooting can be accomplished with one gun and a good stuffer, and this is often faster than a Gun who doesn't normally use a pair, or having a pair but a poor loader. In every respect it's a great deal safer. Safety rules for using a pair are as follows:
1) Practise with your loader, using snap caps
2) Guns will only be passed with the safety catch on safe
3) Make sure that your loader is provided with, and encouraged to wear hearing protection (Health & Safety at Work Act)
4) Never, ever use your wife/husband or a close friend to load or stuff for you. This will certainly lead to arguments, maybe even divorce. When choosing a loader/stuffer always go for one who is shorter than you. For this reason I prefer women, as they are usually shorter and if well trained are better than men because they concentrate and have much nimbler fingers for putting cartridges in guns. Also, they are usually better looking! My present loader, Rosemary Naish ACA, is the best I have ever had, and not only am I always fully loaded, but because she is a chartered accountant I have a running kills-to-cartridges figure, plus a good double check on where birds are down. However, being a keen flyfisher she does insist that all jays are hers!

Preparing for the Season

At the end of the season you, like 95 per cent of my clients, put your gun in its case and forget about it until early July, when you race to the gunsmith only to find he's away, or too busy to get it ready for action in August at the grouse. You will then phone your local shooting school to find that they don't have a space on the day before you go north, which of course is the day your harassed gunsmith has promised the gun for. Proverb 1) a fast gunsmith does not exist; 2) God's wrath is a great deal faster than a good gunsmith; and 3) you are more likely to 'get a cheque in the post' than get your gun back on the day promised.

The correct way of going about the vital preparation for the following season is as follows:-
February 28th: Last day of evening pigeon flighting.
March 1st: Take gun to gunsmith for annual strip-clean, to raise dents in barrels, stock, etc etc. I would suggest that you get a statement as to the completion date (signed in the gunsmith's own blood).

May 1st: Receive the gun back from the gunsmith.

May 2nd: Go to a local gun club and fire, say, fifty cartridges, to ascertain that the trigger pulls the same and that all works well (if not, return to the gunsmith and shoot him in the foot).

June 1st: Book lesson for late June, early July at a local shooting school.

July 1st: Have a shooting lesson at a school to prove that all is well, and book further lessons for mid-August and late-October.

August 15th: Visit shooting school and practise for grouse and partridge.

October 20th: Visit shooting school and practise on a tower for high pheasants.

Three visits to the shooting school are in fact a luxury, and a lot can be done with a clay trap in a farmer's field. Do remember, however, that as this is driven shooting, you must protect the trapper. A few straw bales are not enough, and metal of at least 12g should be used. The high pheasant lesson is wholly necessary and you should book it well in advance as most schools are flat out in the winter months.

A final thought: be confident, trust your natural instincts and enjoy yourself. But *do* remember, 'all the pheasants ever bred, won't repay for one man dead'.

7
Etiquette on the Shooting Day

Over the years there has built up a tradition of practice and custom in the shooting field which all who take part are expected to know. From our earliest years we are taught how to address adults, not to lean our elbows on the table nor speak with mouths full to overflowing. In turn, the cricket pitch and rugby field bring their own customs—the polite clap for an incoming batsman, the solicitous attending to an injured player of the other side, the cheers for the opposition at the end—and it is much the same in the shooting field. He who transgresses reveals himself as both a tyro and one with bad manners.

There are two main criteria for establishing good conduct on a shooting day, be it 'rough' or formal, and they are consideration for others and safety. Learning to be a skilful shot is not difficult for anyone with a hint of aptitude, good hand and eye co-ordination, and a good clay coach, and brilliant Shots discover to their surprise that their skill is not a passport to instant popularity—often the reverse, for such are humans. If that good Shot is seen to be greedy, discourteous or scornful of custom, it would matter not if he performed as well as Lord Walsingham himself: no-one would enjoy his company, and his invitations would dry up a good deal more quickly than they came.

Being considerate makes the world go round; we are in the field to enjoy ourselves and not to be competitive or 'get one up' on the man next door. A sportsman is happy when his friend, guest or companion is getting the chances, whatever his own shots. Friendly rivalry is one thing, but obsessive competition as in Isobel Colgate's *The Shooting Party*, or the modern clay ground where cash prizes go to those who hit most, is not a feature of the covertside. There is room in the shooting field for the inept, the beginner and the downright poor shot, but there is none for the boor who shoots selfishly and breaks the written and unwritten rules of good conduct.

The Duties of the Host

The host as well as the guest has certain obligations, and these include the following:

Sending shooting invitations in good time. A last-minute one risks the guest being booked elsewhere and suggests that he is a last-minute thought or that his invitation is the result of a cancellation. Nobody likes to be considered second choice. If this *is* the case, then come clean and make it clear that someone has dropped out and 'would you possibly be so very kind as to help out by filling the gap . . .' etc.

Giving clear instructions as to how your shoot may be found. Many shooting estates are reached via a maze of minor country roads, through this gateway, down that drive, not at the big house but round the stable yard, near the head keeper's cottage or whatever. To say 'Falconridge Park' and leave a bemused guest—probably short of time and looking at his watch—to hunt 35,000 acres and two villages, is thoughtless. *You* know your way like the back of your hand, but he will not, and might have an anxious start to a day when he ought to be enjoying himself.

Introducing guests to other Guns as they arrive. This is common courtesy but easy to overlook by a shoot captain worried about the day ahead and with a thousand and one things on his mind. However, a newcomer could well feel isolated and alone, and might lack the self-confidence to introduce himself.

Explaining clearly in his opening address what the 'form' for the day will be. All need to know quite clearly what the numbering system is: do you number from the right or left? How many Guns are there? How many places do you advance each drive? Are there to be walking Guns? All needs to be explained, for no two shoots are the same. Some shoots do not shoot foxes, woodcock, hen pheasants (sometimes or always) or any ground game. Your guest will need to know this to save embarrassment. A reminder to even the oldest hand about the safety rules never does any harm, and a warning about low birds, the positions of the pickers-up, the likely appearance of deer, guinea fowl or any other oddity does no harm and makes the guests feel involved.

Doing what he can to make first-time guests or beginners have a shot or two. It is well known that the more you try to help someone who is out of things, Murphy's Law decrees that the fewer chances he has, but a host who knows his ground and enjoys a degree of flexibility can sometimes help by moving people round discreetly so that the sport is fairly shared. Not always easy, but just another thing for a thoughtful host to bear in mind.

Ensuring that the guest receives a decent brace of birds at the end of the day. Check, or make sure your keeper checks, for hard-mouthed dogs, toughness or other damage. On tiny shoots there is sometimes not enough to go round, in which case the FHB—'Family Hangs Back'—rule comes into play.

The Duties of the Guest

However, the guest has the weightier list of responsibilities, although these will come to him as second nature after a while, for he has the greatest incentive of all to get it right—he wants to be asked again; so he becomes a quick learner. But there are pitfalls for the unwary, especially in a world where, through no fault of their own, many enter the sport without the benefit of a proper training from boyhood. This instant guide will save you from the most usual of ghastly bloomers; the rest is down to your own character, common courtesy, social graces and life skills. Thus as a guest you should observe the following conventions:

Answer a shooting invitation as soon as possible. Do not hang back in the hope of something better turning up. And when you have accepted, on no account go back on your word if another invitation appears. If you do, you will discover that the shooting world is, like many specialised fields, a small one and word will get round, so that you will have virtually barred yourself for life from the place of the first invitation. Ask for precise directions, and it might be wise to confirm the engagement a week or so beforehand.

Ask if lunch is to be provided. This is easily overlooked, but a simple question clears the matter up and saves embarrassment—not to mention hunger—if you get it wrong.

Do not take along a spouse or a friend unless you have cleared it in advance. Seating on shoot transport is often tight enough and there may not be enough food for unexpected guests. Some shoot captains have an aversion to companions, specially those dressed in gaudy anoraks who may or may not pass loud and gratuitous comments on the conduct and events of the day. Ask by all means; a polite but firm refusal will make the matter clear.

Do not take your dog unless you have specifically asked if it will be welcome. On most driven shoots the dog work is done by others—pickers-up, beaters and the like. Your dog will not add much to the success of the day for there will not be much for it to do. It takes up room in the waggon and is another thing for you to worry about. Moreover to take an ill-trained dog on someone else's shoot is little short of madness, for nothing peeves a shoot captain more than a guest's dog which is systematically beating out the next drive but one, between bouts of fighting with all the other dogs present. Bad dogs have caused more high blood pressure and lost invitations than almost anything else. If you are staying overnight and your dog is welcome, remember you must make arrangements for kennelling and feeding.

Dress correctly and check before leaving home that you have everything with you. See Chapter 4 for what to wear, but be sure to pack your waterproofs, Wellies and shoes for afterwards, and remember that a hat of some sort is *de rigeur*. To leave behind just one small but vital item can effectively ruin your day, and who wants the embarrassment of asking to borrow?

Take plenty of cartridges. It is far better to take some home unused than to run out. Spare cartons may be taken on the trailer or Guns' waggon, or left back at your car for topping up at lunchtime (though make sure you *will* be going back to your car at lunchtime). Use a leather cartridge bag from which to top up your pockets as required. Do not take a cartridge belt; sorry, but it just looks 'naff' on a formal day and in any case, host and keeper might infer that you were expecting a maximum of only twenty-five shots and feel hurt. Some folk are very sensitive about what to the layman seems the smallest thing. To run out of cartridges is also an implied insult as though you were saying in so many words 'I did not come expecting to shoot many birds here . . .': so, another black mark.

Picking up cartridge cases is a hard one; instinctively you will wish to do it, but if you are the only one, you might be seen to be making too conspicuous a gesture. It is customary on many shoots for cases to be picked up from the pegs by the keeper, if not after every shoot, then regularly during the season. Keep your eyes open and see what the others are doing.

Some large shoots expect double guns, but do not assume this unless told. To be the only one to turn up with doubles might be to embarrass your host. If double guns *are* expected, then you need to find out if a loader is provided or if you bring your own. If the latter, make sure that you have had a little practice together. If you have a single gun on a double gun day, a loader can stand behind and reload your single gun for you—better, in my opinion, than borrowing a pair of ill-fitting and unfamiliar guns just for the day—but this, too, requires practice.

Make sure you arrive in good time. Ten minutes early is so much better than one minute late. Allow yourself time to sort out your equipment, put your gun together, pull on your boots, assess the weather prospects and generally

soak up the atmosphere of what might be a new place. Leave home in good time and allow for getting lost at least once, and you will be about right. As soon as possible, introduce yourself to your host. To rush off and greet a chum whom you happen to spot among the assembling beaters is plain bad manners. So, straight to your host; and if you are not sure which one he is, then ask: he will take care of you thereafter, introduce you to your fellow sportsmen and make you feel welcome.

When it comes to the shooting remember that not everything which passes within range has to be saluted. There is a risk of wounding if you overreach yourself, and you are not there to practise. However, for the future, a lesson or two at the shooting school will be a great help. You owe it to your host, the other guests, the beaters and keeper to do your best and to come with as high a level of proficiency as you can.

Listen carefully to the instructions from the host about what you may and may not shoot; local special rules; the position of stops and pickers-up; and the numbering system, which on some shoots could confuse a professor of mathematics. If in doubt ask, or find, an old hand who knows the ground and check with him. A hastily gabbled: 'Number from the right, advance three between drives, except drive three when you advance two, numbers nine and ten walking each time except for drive one'—can be confusing for anyone with only half an ear on proceedings. The old hands are the ones who remember their numbers after lunch; make sure you are among them!

Make sure of the territorial boundaries between you and your neighbours. To poach a neighbour's shot is considered bad form, and a bird is better spared than shared. By all means call a polite 'Yours' to a neighbour, and he ought to be doing the same to you.

Remember the back Gun: on a shoot with a prolific show of birds, or where you find yourself in a noted prime spot, you might find that a 'back Gun' has been placed some distance behind you. Ostensibly his job is to deal with flushes or birds missed by the chap in front—in this case, you. A sporting Gun will not leave him this rather melancholy role but will allow some good birds through, especially those which, rising late, provide a marginal opportunity of a sporting shot, but the back Gun the chance of a cracker.

A 'shared' bird: it happens sometimes that two neighbouring Guns will fire simultaneously at the same bird—easily done—and often the bird will fall dead. It is impossible to say for certain who killed it, it might have been either of you or indeed both. A sportsman will congratulate the man next to him on a good shot, even when certain that *he* was on target.

It is better not to boast: like many sports, shooting can harbour an element of oneupmanship, and there is a temptation for the young, the over-excited or the callow to resort to boasting about the number of birds they have shot. The late Robert Churchill observed, 'Never point out to others how well or badly you are shooting: *they will have noticed!'* Enough said!

Keep quiet when moving to position; game is not deaf and will take evasive action the moment it hears that humans are in the offing. Remain silent and creep to your position. You will notice the loud people in the field, how their raucous shouts and guffaws drift down the wind from great distances and sully the morning freshness. Notice, too, how rarely game seems to fly in their direction.

As a beginner and thus probably also one green in years, *have a thought for those longer in the tooth.* Common courtesy might be at a rare commodity in the jolly bustle of the current age, but in the shooting field I am pleased to report that vestiges of it may still be found. Help old-timers over rough places, offer to hold their guns, do not rush to the best seat in the shoot vehicle, or stride ahead over heavy plough in your seven-league boots while trying to hold a conversation with a man old enough to be your grandfather whose legs are not what they were forty years ago.

It is a strict rule not to load your gun until you arrive at your peg, and to unload it as soon as the drive is over. A whistle or horn will sound the beginning and end of the action, and it is only during this period that you may shoot. After the whistle has gone, it is not unusual for a glorious cock pheasant or a woodcock which has hung on until positively the last minute, to rise perversely and present a lovely chance. Resist temptation and do not fire. Between drives your gun should be carried broken at the breech or in a closed gunslip. The latter is not proof of absolute safety as there is no guarantee that the gun was not placed already loaded in the slip, and soft

Guns making their way to the next drive should proceed quietly, dogs at heel and guns safely in slips. The keeper does not appreciate loud conversation, loose dogs or straying humans which might disturb the next drive

leather is scant protection against an accidental discharge. However, this consideration appears not to bother the great majority of shoot captains.

Your good training will have taught you *to avoid not only unsafe but also unsporting birds,* those which fly low or are obviously immature. You will find that standards vary from shoot to shoot as to what they consider acceptable, but I am saying that some standards should be universal, and a poor bird here is a poor bird anywhere. It is easy to be tempted, especially if you are surrounded by those whom you feel should know better, but who seem to derive a curious satisfaction from knocking down head-high, half-feathered poults which you could have hit with a tennis racquet.

Notice where your wounded birds come down: on a good driven day it might be that you have a number of birds down after the end of a drive. It is important that you make it a rule to remember where each one is. A picker-up will come up and ask, 'Anything to pick?' An old hand will be able to reply, 'Two by the firs, one runner by the willow, three dead just inside the wood and a partridge in the tussocks out in front'. Such is the mark of an expert and something to which the beginner should aspire.

It is bad form to leave obviously wounded birds flapping about in full view of the onlookers. If no-one is to hand to come to your help and you have no dog, then choose your moment, unload your gun, set it down and, provided it is safe to do so, go quickly to dispatch the wounded bird, rather than add to your tally whilst it suffers.

Tipping is part of the ritual of the occasion and a small way of saying 'Thank you' to the keeper who has worked to give you the best day he can. Often his wages are set at a level which takes account of gratuities. The tip should be given at the end of the day when you are presented with your brace. Do not wave the money in the air and make much of your generosity, but slip it to him in such a way that no-one but you and he are aware that it has taken place; it can usually be combined with a handshake.

The rule of thumb is a minimum of £10.00 for up to 100 head, and a minimum of £5.00 for each 100 thereafter. This figure will depend on your financial circumstances, and while it is not a good idea to give more than you can afford, it is equally shortsighted to be stingy. The keeper should not be held to blame for bad weather, poor shooting or anything which is beyond his control. As well as thanking the keeper, thank any beaters who are still around; they appreciate it. Sad to say that some shooting parties have a reputation among beaters for arrogance, a label all too often well deserved. A surprising number of Guns fail even to greet the beaters in the morning when they pass them in the farmyard. A friendly word makes all the difference.

If you have been given a loader, unlikely in your early days but not impossible, she/he ought to be tipped too, as should the person who cleans your gun for you; some hosts offer this as part of their hospitality.

It is important to say goodbye to your fellow sportsmen, shaking them each by the hand, leaving your host until last and thanking him most warmly for the day. Anyone who has given you a day's shooting has bestowed a gift of great value. In the event of a shoot supper, watch the amount you drink, (nothing if you are to drive), and do not overstay your welcome.

The very next morning write your host a letter of thanks. In my view a telephone call will not do. The letter need be neither long nor fulsome, but should simply thank him again for a most enjoyable day, mention one particular highlight maybe, and thank him for his hospitality.

This list might seem formidable and much to remember, particularly as you are there to enjoy yourself. However, much of it is common courtesy and the underlying theme is sportsmanship. A good sportsman is equally happy to see others enjoying themselves and having a pleasant day: if you stick to that maxim, and if everyone is as considerate as you, your shooting days will be things to cherish in the memory. The greedy, competitive and selfish never enjoy themselves; they make few friends and find that their invitations dry up a good deal faster than they came. It would be nice to think that your host is happy to invite you back.

Your First Game Shoot

A major milestone in the life of the young Shot is that longed-for invitation to the first 'proper' shoot. One moment you are at peace with the world pottering about your humble affairs, and then the telephone shrills. It is the farmer from the estate down the road, the place where you had permission to shoot pigeons and rabbits. 'Doing anything on Saturday?' Whatever it was you were planning is cancelled in an instant, but you do not wish to appear over-eager. 'Er, no . . . I think I'm free . . .'. 'Good; I was wondering if you'd like to come and shoot with us; someone has dropped out at the last minute, and I knew you wouldn't mind my asking at late notice . . . just a small day with a few friends, all driven of course. Bring a sandwich; meet in the yard at 9.15; supper afterwards'. You are barely able to stammer a few poor words of thanks, and that is it. Sudden turmoil; your head is a'buzz with unarticulated hopes, fears and the promise of wild dreams come true.

Your pride is wounded not at all by the thought that you are filling in for a cancellation, for nothing can sully your pure delight. Your arduous apprenticeship is finally served, all that plinking with the air rifle in the early days, the first single-barrelled .410 and then the 12; the stalked rabbits, pigeons and magpies, helping the keeper with a fox drive, or tagging along with the smallholders on their monthly clay shoot. At last, the real test is here.

Indeed, all those pleasures will still be there when you return, for they are everlasting, no matter how much shooting you do; and now the formal driven shoot, elevated almost to an art form in the UK, is about to become part of your experience, along with all those written and unwritten rules, designed, it seems, to trap the unwary and the ignorant—this means you!

Although it ought not to top the list of your priorities, for some reason the matter of your appearance assumes great importance. You must conform to the convention of the field and also make allowances for the worst the British winter weather can do. To turn out in your old 'kammo' pigeoning gear or muddy wildfowling overalls is not the thing, unless you wish to cause offence to host and fellow Guns. As a beginner you may not yet aspire to a pair of breeks, and while you will need them sooner rather than later, for the time being it will be acceptable to wear ordinary trousers (not jeans) of neutral colour tucked into socks and then Wellies (which do not *have* to be green ones).

Dark shirt and neck-tie with body warmer or sweater, topped off with a waxproof coat will complete the ensemble, not forgetting the hat, without which no shooting man is properly dressed. Mittens should be taken if the weather is cold: you may have to wait for some time in an exposed place. All clothing should be of sober and natural colours; no white shirts or fluorescent anoraks.

Resist the temptation to cut a dash by taking along the accoutrements and family heirlooms used by your ancestors. The leather hip flask and brass-bound shooting stick may look impressive but they can get in the way and ought to be left to your elders. Take a good lot of cartridges, a bagful—you can always bring the unfired ones home again, for to run out is discourteous to your host; it infers you had underestimated the quality of sport he had to offer. Pick up your empty cases, no matter what other people might do. Your packed lunch should be simple and filling, and should include a flask of hot soup or coffee. Do not leave it on the kitchen table, the last resting place of all too many shooting lunches. Supper was promised, so you need a change of footwear to avoid having to pass the evening in stockinged feet, and a clean sweater or jacket to wear when you discard your wet and muddy shooting clothes.

When the great day dawns, you are up betimes after a sleepless night so are not likely to be late, but do not arrive too early. Ten minutes or so before the allotted time is about right; this gives you the chance to collect your gear and put your gun together and deal with any unexpected hitches. On no account will you have brought your trusty shooting dog unless specifically invited to do so. There will be other dogs there, and yours will prove an encumbrance unless it is trained to Field Trial standards.

On arrival you will see a mêlée of men, dogs and boys, and possibly even some ladies. A good host will have watched for your arrival, but should he have missed you, seek him out *before* you embark on a long conversation with a chum whom you recognise among the beaters. Your host will introduce you to your fellow Guns—he will probably reel off a list of names and you will find it hard to recall a single one of them at the end. Try to remember one or two: Mr Brown, beard; Mr Jenkins, deerstalker hat; and they will act as focal points. 'The Gun on the left of Mr Brown', is a nice try. I scribble key names down on a piece of paper when no-one is looking and secretly consult it from time to time.

Bid a cheery 'Good Morning!' to the beaters. You may see friends there, but today you are a Gun rather than a beater and your place is with the former—though remember you are not the Duke of Plaza Toro and your demeanour should be polite and pleasant to all. The host will call the Guns together at the appointed time; pay heed to the instructions. Basically this will concern what you can or cannot shoot; no ground game is a common rule, or no hen pheasants, no foxes, or whatever. You will draw your peg number and be told that you line out from right to left, up to eight (or nine, or ten), and you advance two (or three) per drive with the last number walking each time. There will be variations dictated by local custom, so pay close attention and remember what you have been told: your host will only say it once! The old hands are the Guns who can remember their numbers after lunch; it would be nice were you to be among them. It goes without saying that you will be between the same two fellow sportsmen all day.

Then you are off, walking with your gun in its slip, on your way to the first stand on your very first driven shoot. As you proceed, do not boast of your feats with the rabbits and pigeons; nobody will be impressed and in any case, the rule of silence on the way to the peg is a wise one, never mind if there is a chatterbox among you. Start as you mean to continue. You will find that marksmanship is deemed less important than safety, modesty and a sportsmanlike attitude: those are what you will be remembered for.

At your peg, dump on the ground your cartridge bag, take the gun from the slip and, if necessary, stamp a small level place on which to stand, useful if you are on some ploughing. Take your favourite (only?) gun from its slip, and do *not* as I did once, borrow a posh sidelock for the occasion, just for the sake of appearances. It belonged to a man 6 feet 6 inches tall and I was 5 feet 10! Pride pinches! I hope your usual gun is a conventional over-and-under or side-by-side; a single barrel is too limited, and there is still prejudice against semi-autos and pumps, even though they may have been converted to the three-shot option.

Find out the precise position of your neighbours; if one is half-hidden by a bush make sure you have seen each other and have acknowledged the fact by a wave of the hand. Behind will be pickers-up, standing quietly and unobtrusively by the far hedge; you will fire no low shots behind, but you need to ascertain where they are. Stops will be standing in the hedge, possibly quite close to you, and you will hear their steady tapping which prevents birds leaking out along the arteries of the woodlands.

The whistle or horn which shrills out to signal the start of the drive sets your adrenalin flowing: now you may shoot. You load the gun, bringing stock to barrels when shutting the breech and, adopting one of the accepted postures, face the direction you expect birds to come. Early blackbirds will come shrieking alarm round the woodside, and showers of small birds will scatter through the tree tops—but do not be tempted to have a go at the early crow or impossibly high pigeon.

You are torn between the desire for a shot and the fervent hope that nothing will come near you and expose your shortcomings; but what the heck! You are there to enjoy yourself and we cannot all be brilliant. Worry not! An early pheasant comes with a clatter and a chortle, neatly killed by a

man down the line. On no account will you so much as aim your gun over the heads of neighbours, even if a bird flies that way. That is known as shooting 'down the line' and is dangerous. Dismount the gun and pick up the target behind after it has passed by.

A bird comes halfway between you and the Gun on your left (Smithson, pipe), and wisely you leave it for him. He scrambles it down and raises his hat to you in recognition of your good manners: Brownie points earned. Another bird comes to your left and you resist the urge to shout a warning of its approach, a common fault. Now it is your turn: a cock pheasant rises somewhere in the middle of the wood, corkscrews up to tree-top height and heads your way, veering neither to right nor left. Suddenly the moment is upon you, your tensions fade and for that moment you are alone, out there with your pigeons and rabbits. Effortlessly the gun finds the shoulder, the shot rings out, the head of the bird folds back and it thumps with complete and exhilarating finality on the grass behind. What a moment!

'Good shot!' you hear Smithson (pipe, remember?) from next door. Hit or miss—all one in the end, but very important indeed when you are starting. The old saying 'What's hit is history, what's missed, mystery' still holds good. At the end of the drive a picker-up might come and ask 'Anything to pick, Sir?' and you must be ready to tell him the precise place where a wounded bird might have gone down, or where a dead bird has fallen in cover. An airy wave of the hand at a distant one hundred-acre block of scrub woodland is not good enough. He wants to know by which bush it went down, and his job is hard enough already without your making it more difficult.

When the whistle has blown to signal the end of the drive, unload your gun and put it in its slip or carry it broken over your arm. Never fire at anything else, no matter how tempting, until the signal for the start of the next drive has sounded. Thus the day progresses. Your fellow Guns will be observing your performance as well as that of each other, so there is no need for you to point out to them how well or how badly you are doing for they will have noticed it themselves. You learn that in the shooting field you can get away with very little; whatever you do, someone, somewhere will have seen it.

Confine your remarks to complimenting others on good shots, or commiserate for bad luck, and hope that they will do as much for you. Lend old-timers a hand as they struggle through inadequate gaps, and in general put the pleasure of your companions before that of yourself: be modest and polite, and learn that praise is harder to handle than criticism.

Thus passes your first shoot, and you come to relax and gain an inkling of the thrills, the excitement, the effort that has gone into making your day enjoyable. You might learn something of the problems of shoot organisation and of gamekeeping. At the end, as you stand chatting, the keeper will come up with a brace of birds selected for their lack of damage and youthful good looks. Slip your tenner into his hand as you shake it and thank him for his hard work. He has put in ten months hard graft so that you might have a day of pleasure today.

Write your thank you letter the following morning, and hope that you have shown yourself the sort of person whom your host of the day before would like to invite again. If you have failed to get it right and for some reason are not asked back, you may never know why. Such is the last and most quirky of the unwritten laws of the formal shoot.

8
The Shoot Captain

This functionary is the closest the shooting man comes to the Almighty. In the field on a shooting day his word is law, and it is he who makes the decisions; the mightiest in the land come and go at his bidding, and thus he can send a duke to walk in a field of wet kale or an admiral to struggle over sixty acres of heavy ploughing. He may commandeer your vehicle, change plans at short notice and do as he pleases, for this man is a despot, a king for a day and upon his shoulders rests the ultimate responsibility. Much is spoken about shooting days being run by gamekeepers, and I do not hold with it: the guv'nor is the man, and anyone who would allow his servant to organise his affairs makes an error. Keepers who boast that it is they and not their masters who run things ought to be shown the door.

The shoot captain has much to plan in advance. He must issue his invitations in good time, especially if his guests have full shooting diaries. Saturdays are sometimes difficult as many shoot on that day, if only to guarantee a supply of beaters; so if you shoot on a Saturday you must issue invitations early, possibly during the summer before the season.

The selection should be made carefully, for a shooting day is also a social occasion. You would not invite to dinner those who had little in common or who were likely to be antagonistic, and it is much the same on a shoot. Some hosts issues invitations on a theme: those who live locally, the very young, or those who have met on some other non-shooting occasions and got on well. The guests should be carefully matched.

To shoot or not to shoot is dictated by the amount of game on the land. On a wild bird shoot this is critical, as he does not wish to erode his stock and over-kill his shootable surplus. He should know what sort of day to plan, and if he is good at his job, how to regulate the size of the bag by selecting suitable drives and gun placements. On a reared shoot he has none of those worries, but he still needs to eke his birds out through a long season; and while not allowing too many to be killed on one day, he must show his guests a reasonable quality and quantity of game.

He plans drives with the keeper or head beater well in advance. They discuss the placing of stops, pickers-up, the movement of personnel from here to there, the handling of the game, drivers of vehicles and the provision of refreshment. Some tasks he may delegate, but he is still in charge and therefore responsible if things should go wrong. It is likely that the shoot layout will be familiar to both keeper and beater, so the drives may not take long to plan; but if the weather appears set to ruin it and you reverse drives, are you *certain* there is a plank across that wide ditch?

Transport is usually arranged by liaising with the farmer unless the shoot has special vehicles of its own. Drivers should be experienced, or farm workers familiar with towing unless the insurance is to be invalidated. The days when any lad could hop on a tractor and drive a load of the gentry down a rutted roadway have gone for good. All farm and shoot insurance should be up to date, and it is a wise rule that all who shoot with you are fully covered for third party injury. Membership of BASC or of the BFSS covers this.

If food is to be laid on, be sure it is properly done, that the providers are properly briefed and the quantities monitored. Is the lunch place clean and swept? At what time do you want the meal served? How is payment to be made? All such points and more have to be covered. Your views about the usefulness of shoot helpers should be made known to the keeper or head beater, as should the numbers of helpers for whom you have budgeted and a review of the going rate of pay. Pay packets should be made up in advance in named envelopes; it saves a lot of fuss at the end of the day.

By the evening of the shoot all these preparations will have been put in hand, and if your attention to detail has been thorough enough there should be no last-minute panics. Be ready for the unexpected, though. A last-minute bout of 'flu for a Gun or key helper can give you a nasty half-hour on the phone, and a sudden change in the weather, such as eight inches of snow, can make you go a little thoughtful; but barring such accidents, your head should fall to the pillow clear of anxieties that things will go anything but smoothly.

You will be up betimes, possibly driving round the shoot keeping an eye on the woods, seeing where the game is moving and watching for disturbance such as dog walkers or joggers. You will be at the point of assembly early, in time to welcome the guests. Make it a point to be the first to speak to newcomers—they will seek you out, but make yourself available to them and try to avoid involved conversations with the keeper or another guest. Introduce guests to other Guns and make them feel at home and welcome. Tell them at what time you expect to move off so there should be no unseemly rush. The great art is to make it all appear easy, and not to communicate anxiety to others for it is a contagious ailment.

You may need to get your beating team moving early if some blanking in needs to be done, and a word to the keeper might be necessary. In the event of a Gun being late (sometimes delays are inevitable no matter how early people set off), you will have to decide how long *you* can wait without spoiling the day for the others. You might have to move off and leave a lad behind to show the latecomer which way to go. In my experience late arrivals are not common; those who manage to arrive late for work seem somehow never to do the same for a day's shooting! Once you have assembled, call all the Guns round for *the bollocking!*

It is most important that the initial address to the Guns is given clearly in a way which all can understand, so there is no confusion. It is useful if the captain has a written list to make sure that all points are covered and none left out. The newcomers may be introduced again to the assembled throng. A brief outline of the plan for the day is a good idea: *you* may know exactly what is to happen, where you are going and that you plan to slip in a

Game-carrying strap for a picker-up is handier than a bag

GRAND PRIX PARIS
BY SPECIAL APPOINTMENT TO
BY SPECIAL APPOINTMENT TO
KING OF ITALY
H.R.H. THE PRINCE OF
HOLLAND &
Gun & Rifle
98, NEW BOND
HOLLAND 6
&
6

Old but good; English game guns are the best in the world

The picker-up needs only one bird to justify his role

partridge drive halfway through the morning, but the others do not, so share these plans with them—they will feel more involved. People like to know how many drives are planned and what time lunch is.

Make it quite clear what may and may not be shot. The rule of the day might be cocks only, one hen per gun per drive, no ground game (this is a common one), or no foxes—but whatever it is, make it crystal clear so that there may be no slip-ups and subsequent embarrassment. A word about safety never does any harm, no matter how experienced the team; the old and complacent are often the ones at greatest risk and a reminder about leaving low birds and the fact that pickers-up are lurking somewhere behind, will help to concentrate their minds.

Early on you will organise the draw for positions. Your position-finder of whatever sort, be it engraved metal goblets, plastic tags, ivory pegs—there are some beautiful and unusual variations—will have been prepared in advance and offered to the Guns, guests first. As each takes his number, get him to say it, and repeat it yourself; confusion between 6 and 9 can occur, and even at that early stage it is not unknown for someone to forget before you have even moved off! It may seem fussy, but attention to detail is the secret of success.

Each shoot has its own system of progression from peg to peg after each drive so that the shooting may be shared fairly. The one or two high number Guns might walk with the beaters and act as flankers. Most, but not all shoots number from right to left; some advance two pegs per drive, others three; sometimes a minor drive might not count as a full drive so that Guns do not advance at the end of it but keep their numbers. The possible variations are endless, and it is clearly of great importance that your guests understand your own rules, which may be perfectly familiar to you, but potentially confusing for someone hearing them for the first time.

Having made all clear, and having asked for and dealt with any questions, you may invite the Guns to move off to the waiting transport or to walk to the first drive. Your own role thereafter will be to assume a low profile. No-one wishes to see you leaping about, but discreetly you move here and there, the man with the oil-can. You help someone find a peg that might have been knocked down; you indicate the position of the pickers-up where this would be helpful: you act as an impromptu stop should you see pheasants moving in directions they ought not to be taking. Keep your eye on your watch and control the pace of the day by quietly moving on the sluggardly, curbing the over-eager, seeing that unruly dogs are controlled, and generally keeping up the spirits of the team, much as would a host at a party. You can jolly folk along without being bossy or giving offence, but still in a subtle manner, getting your own way. That is the trick.

Accidents rarely happen nowadays, thank goodness, but it pays to know what to do in the event of one. Even on the best shoots a pellet has been known to lodge by accident in the flesh of a human or canine bystander, and sometimes even worse can happen. You are in charge, the rest will look to you for a lead. First-aid materials should always be available in the beaters' waggon or on the Guns' cart. If necessary send a swift messenger for the ambulance, making sure it is someone who knows the ground and can give an accurate description of where you are.

In the event of an odd pellet ending up where it should not, you have no option but to ask the culprit to leave the field immediately. This is expected, and you cannot ask the rest to run the risk of someone who has proved himself unsafe. Post mortems may come later, but at the time do not over-dramatise the event; speak quietly and privately to the culprit, and do all you can to keep everyone calm. Unless the accident is serious it ought to be possible to continue with the day's sport. Your shoot rule is that all Guns are covered by third party insurance; however, it is better by far to ensure by your own organisation and careful selection of guests that the chances of an accident are reduced to a minimum: they can never be reduced to nil.

It is far more likely that you might have to deal with a complaint of a dangerous shot, or some other breach of the rules. Some Guns will deal with such matters themselves but many more will report it to you. If you have been doing your job and are aware of what is going on—a shoot captain develops eyes in the back of his head—you will have seen the low shot or the down-the-line swing which has caused the trouble. Quite calmly seek out the offender at a suitable moment, and *in private* point out what he did wrong and make it clear in no uncertain terms that it is unacceptable. This may be done firmly but without rancour, and in such a way as not to make an enemy but nonetheless to have the desired effect.

This is a disagreeable aspect of what is otherwise a fascinating and responsible job, but it has to be mastered and with luck it will not happen all that often. If the offender repeats his error your problem is whether or not to send him home—rather drastic, you might think, but if a dangerous Shot remains and there is a serious accident thereafter, your diffidence will have been directly responsible for a serious injury or, Heaven forbid, fatality. It would be ironic to arrive at the pearly gates with the explanation that you always knew George was a dangerous shot, but you did not care to hurt the old boy's feelings: what an epitaph! As shoot captain *you* are responsible for the safety of all those present, and sometimes responsibility means being tough, even when it hurts.

The great art is to run the day so well that nobody is aware that you are involved; unobtrusive management is the best sort, backed up by uncompromisingly high standards. At the end of the day all is not over. The beaters and pickers-up must be paid; your preparations of the night before and the made-up pay packets will save you some time here. Some shoots prefer to pay their people at lunchtime which allows them to get off home at the end of the afternoon and not be kept hanging about at a time when the shoot captain has a great deal on his mind. Alternatively, the paying may be left to the keeper or head beater who hired the helpers and knows them individually; doing this will reinforce his authority.

Game cards must be written out. This job may be delegated, but it has to be done by somebody. Many shoots have their own card and one each must be prepared for all who shot there that day, and handed out before they go home. It looks a bit 'off' to have the Guns searching for scraps of paper, borrowing pens and trying in failing light to make a note of the bag on the back of a cigarette packet. It is a matter of detail, and such small courtesies are important and make the difference between a good and an indifferent day.

You are responsible for the game, and will have delegated the hanging of the bag and the selection of birds for the Guns, each of whom expects a brace of carefully selected pheasants, partridges or grouse to take home. This is the job of the keeper but you must be sure that it is done properly. The keeper may expect to receive his tip from the Gun at that moment and he should not be deprived of it. The sale of surplus game must also be dealt with. Big shoots often have a contract with a game dealer who will come by arrangement and collect the whole of the bag, which might represent a significant part of shoot income. You may have neighbouring farmers, tenants or locals you need to thank for keeping an eye on the place, or for many of the other little favours which oil the wheels of any shoot. Pheasants make a suitable present, so remember to hold back so many brace.

Smaller shoots will often sell the bag privately, so the shoot captain ought to have a game dealer's licence renewable annually and available from his local District Council. Beaters will often buy birds, and the recent trend of falling game prices makes them an attractive purchase.

The shoot captain should see that all are happy at the end of the day, and only then bid his guests farewell. The guest should leave with a rosy glow of contentment and his brace of birds, conscious that his day has been carefully orchestrated and his path before him made smooth by good management.

Some shoots extend the hospitality to the après-shoot meal which might be in the house or the pub. The shoot captain's role is extended in this case, and he must see to his guests' needs. Sometimes speeches are made, with thanks to the host and toasts for guests or other luminaries; again the shoot captain has a role. At the end of the evening, after the last tail-lights have glowed red in the drive, he should write up the estate game book while events are still fresh in his mind. This is an important record and must be kept up to date, with seasonal running totals maintained. This information is of interest for its own sake and useful as a record of progress and changing times, but it will also be needed in the event of the shoot being sold or the rights changing hands.

The next day I like to go round with the dog and try to pick any runners which were lost the day before. Even the best pickers-up will lose the odd bird, and if you shoot on a Saturday it makes a good way of passing a Sunday morning to work a dog in the thickets. Do not expect to pick many, but every one found is a bonus. A post mortem with the keeper may be helpful, a view on what went well or badly and how to change things for next time. Shoot vehicles must be tidied, and the game larder swept out; and then you find it is time to plan the next shoot.

The shoot captain is a busy as well as an important man.

9
The Keeper's Year

by Mike Swan

I suppose the keeper's year starts in February. With the last cock day over, another game season ends. The guns get a thorough clean, and perhaps go off to the gunsmith for their annual service. The boss meanwhile turns his attention to other things. It could be what are euphemistically known as 'spring' salmon, complete with ice forming in the rod rings; or it could skiing. Either way, with the season over, minds tend to stray from game. But not for the keeper, whose year starts in earnest again right away—if he has not got his plans together by now, next season will not happen.

So what of the keeper's year? Let us examine in greater detail what it takes to fulfil this most sought-after profession. There are so many different images. To the Gun he is the person in smart matching tweeds who holds the shoot day together; to the game he is the provider of sustenance and cover; and to at least one small boy in the village he is 'A feller who lazes about the country wi' a gun under his arm and a dog at heel'. Sadly, this last romantic image leads many youngsters to believe that the keepering to which they aspire will be an easy and rewarding life: in truth, most keepers face long hours of often lonely work.

Add to this the fact that they are out in all weathers, and often live in remote places which makes a social life difficult for them and even more so for their families, and you realise that keepering is not quite the idyllic lifestyle that might be imagined. However, it does have tremendous rewards in terms of job satisfaction for the right personality.

Perhaps the greatest reward of all is the knowledge that by his actions the keeper is making a real contribution to the conservation of our wonderful countryside. Whether it be heather moorland with its grouse, merlins and golden plover; woods with their butterflies and songbirds; or marshes with their duck and dragonflies, the keeper is constantly enhancing the real countryside. Sad then, that the ignorant still attack keepers in both words and deeds, when our countryside would be so much duller without them and their contribution.

The proof of how much the work of the keeper is conservation-orientated is often manifested more in February than in any other month, for this is the time when the keeper concentrates on improving the habitat of his charges.

The keeper will go round his laying pen regularly to collect eggs which he will find lying about on the ground or laid in rudimentary nests. These eggs will be set in an incubator

The case of the hill keeper, with grouse as his main concern, gives a good example. Grouse rely on heather of mixed ages, young shoots for food and older plants for cover and nesting, and they need the two types in close proximity so that broods of chicks can hide rapidly if danger should present itself. To achieve this, the keeper burns small patches and strips of heather each year in winter and early spring, thus ensuring that every grouse territory on his moor has the right mix of vegetation.

In doing this, he helps to prevent invasion of the ground by poor grasses and other species and ensures that the heather remains vigorous and healthy. This is good for a range of other wildlife, too, of which the diminutive merlin is a special example. This tiny bird of prey lives mainly on the smaller songbirds of the moors, and is in decline due to the loss of its habitat. Where grouse and hill keepering flourish, so does the merlin, but elsewhere it is having an extremely hard time in the face of the overgrazing and afforestation of our precious uplands.

The pheasant keeper does his bit in February too, for this is the season when his birds take least of his time. The breeding stock will be safely penned, and the wild pheasants will be sorting out their territories in copse, field and hedge. With no eggs or chicks to worry about, the keeper can devote himself to improving his woods and coverts.

Perhaps with the aid of his local Game Conservancy adviser, he will walk his ground at this coldest and bleakest time of year, and identify which coverts need improving. With the almost total demise of the hurdle-maker

One of the most significant developments in the control of corvids on the shoot has been the Larsen trap. A captive decoy attracts crows or magpies defending a territory early in the nesting season. All corvids are thieves of ground-nesting birds' eggs, and the eggs and nestlings of garden birds

and because small woodlands have little other use, the copses of southern Britain are fast heading towards dereliction. Only the pheasant and the sport which it offers give a real incentive to maintaining coppice rotations, and hence the diversity of our lowland woods.

And so the keeper, perhaps aided by a few trusty helpers, sets to work with bill hook and chainsaw, and cuts little patches of hazel in his woods. In this way, just like the hill keeper with his heather, he produces woodland at different stages of growth, a mix of age structures and thus a variety of habitats. And as the Game Conservancy has shown, this is good for an enormous range of wildlife, particularly butterflies and many of our migrant songbirds. Again, it is species which are in national and even international decline which are often helped most by this activity.

As February moves into March and April, the days lengthen and the new growth of spring begins. This is the time when insects begin to come out of hibernation, and new growth appears on so much of our plant life. Concomitant with these new stirrings of life is more and richer food for the keeper's charges, and this precipitates the breeding season for game.

As the first eggs are hidden in heather, hedgerow and copse, so the predators move in to hunt this new, nutritious source of food. For the keeper this is the season of greatest danger for his birds: if he does not take action to curb the activities of the predators, there will be few wild gamebirds to provide sport next autumn.

Today's keeper, however, has a far more enlightened view of predation and predator control than his grandfather did. Long gone are the days of ruthless persecution of everything that might conceivably kill a gamebird or its egg or chick. Today's keeper concentrates on the perfectly legal practice of trapping and shooting those key predators which do serious harm to his game. Thus amongst the mammals he works on rats, stoats, foxes and the alien mink; for this spring period, from March to June, he will be hard at work to remove crows and magpies from his area, and other lesser predators will receive his attention if they get out of hand. The grey squirrel, another alien import, can be a serious egg thief and will often damage new woodland habitats such as the keeper has tried to create. For the hill keeper, black-backed gulls can be a real menace as they quarter his moor all summer long in search of growing grouse chicks.

With the intensity of modern farming, predation control alone, even in areas with a great deal of suitable habitat, is rarely able to produce enough wild pheasants to justify driven shooting. Shortage of insects means that chick survival is lower than it used to be, and as a consequence most lowland keepers have to rear and release at least some birds to supplement the wild population. Thus at the same time as he attends to his daily trap rounds, the keeper will probably be managing a laying pen or two to produce his own eggs.

And so it is that on April Fools' day the summer treadmill usually begins, for this is often the date on which the first hen pheasants lay their first eggs. Perhaps they are trying to say something to their keeper! Within two weeks the trickle increases to a flood as the bulk of the birds come into lay, and the keeper can then expect an egg from each hen on four days out of five.

Fortunately they do not all choose the same day on which they fail to lay, so the keeper simply collects about eight eggs for every ten hens each day.

Today more and more keepers send their eggs off, carefully washed and graded and in weekly batches, to be incubated at a game farm. This saves them the worry of running incubators, saves their employer from the capital investment of buying them, and means that they do not have weekly batches of young chicks to deal with. In return the game farmer sends back one or perhaps two larger groups of newly hatched chicks, so the keeper does not have to rear six or eight different age groups when there would be far more bullying if they were mixed together.

And so as May turns into June, the last eggs find their way to the incubators, and the keeper releases his breeding stock, which he hopes will rear a small brood in the wild if the summer is good. At the same time he can afford to ease down the predation control campaign, particularly against the crow family since there will be no more eggs for them to rob.

At this time he will be concentrating mainly on his rearing field, out early in the midsummer dawn to let his birds out into their runs, and back at sunset trying desperately to shut them back into the safety of the huts in case of a cold wet night. This last struggle is made all the more frantic by the fact that dusk and closing time at the local are roughly the same in mid-June, and if you have been on the go since 4am a good pint really is welcome by 10 at night!

Given an ordinary British summer the keeper never has a moment's rest at this time. He needs to have his birds out if the weather is fine, to help them grow up fit and strong for the wild. However, he must get them back under cover if rain threatens, as otherwise they may chill and huddle in a group, when those at the bottom of the pile will suffocate. Why it is that pheasants seem to be hell-bent on suicide from the moment of hatching no-one knows, but it certainly tries the keeper's patience!

In a few brief weeks the birds will be old enough to release back into the wild. So the keeper must rush from rearing field to release sites to prepare these for the arrival of the adolescent pheasants. Fences must be made tall and strong enough both to confine the pheasants and to keep out marauding foxes and mink. Feeding sites must be established, water supplies arranged, and cover provided if there is not enough by way of natural foliage and undergrowth.

By now the keeper will also be thinking about the shooting which is to follow. It may be several months until November, but the best beaters and pickers-up are in high demand; if he does not agree his shooting dates with the boss and book the necessary help by midsummer, he has little chance of finding any of the good ones still free. One Dorset keeper found this to his cost, when moving late to a new job. He finally resorted to numbering his beaters as well as his Guns, and gave each one a peg at the start of the drive with an arrow showing him in which direction to go, and another at the end to ensure that he arrived at the right destination. Sadly it still did not work, as the tortoise and the hare syndrome prevailed with the result that some were through the thicket almost before the others had started!

Meanwhile, with the arrival of July, the grouse keeper will be off to the hill for a sample count of his birds. A careful search across the hill with dogs will find and flush each covey in turn. At this time of year the young 'cheepers' are flying well but are still easy to distinguish from the adults, so the keeper can rapidly assess how many young birds he has with each old pair. There will, of course, be variations: some will have a covey of six or eight or maybe more, but others will have lost the lot; there will also be the single cocks whose hen has been taken on the nest. Knowing what stock he had at the start, the keeper will now be able to decide how many can be shot, and thus whether the pre-planned shooting programme can be adhered to or extended, or indeed whether it will need to be cut.

And so, while the moorland keeper begins his final run-down to the Glorious Twelfth, his low-ground counterpart moves steadily on with the busiest time of all. There may be a few late chicks on the rearing field well into August, but the majority of his hand-reared stock will now be in pens where they need daily attention to check on their welfare as they acclimatise to the rigours of the wild.

The keeper's aim is to manipulate his birds so that by the first shooting day they will be widely spread over the shoot, but still on his own ground, not having strayed over the boundaries. They must also be strong, fit and well feathered, so that they fly as well as the truly wild birds.

August also brings with it the school holidays, and thus the worst time of year for casual trespass. With warm summer days and wild woods to explore, school children not unnaturally go a-wandering. Many will stray from the marked footpaths, and they can cause serious disruption to the birds. Provided, however, that there is no really malicious damage the modern keeper will be reasonably tolerant. He may have to chase a few away from his most vulnerable places, but harmless wandering will not bother

The release pen in high summer is a busy place. On the success of this part of
the rearing operation depends the quantity of sport the following season. In
hot weather the regular topping up of water drinkers can be a chore

The keeper moves his aviary birds in a special coop which allows air to
circulate but is dark enough and just sufficiently cramped to prevent the birds
panicking. Pheasants must be handled gently but firmly at all times

him unduly. One Essex keeper who had more than his fair share of trouble
came up with a novel solution a few years ago. Once school was back, he
rang up the headmaster and invited him to send out classes to see the work
of the local gamekeeper. Given an insight into what was going on, the
youngsters took an interest, and the odd incidents of minor vandalism
stopped. Disturbance of hedges during the nesting season ceased too, and
then the local radio station got to hear of things. Within a few weeks the
keeper concerned was giving regular natural history broadcasts, and
helping to spread the word about the good works of gamekeepers.

As we move into September, the 'season of mists and mellow
fruitfulness', the pheasants will really begin to wander and spread out, and
fine autumn mornings will see them foraging up every sunny hedgerow,
gathering the wild fruits of autumn and heading steadily for the boundary.
At this time, therefore, the keeper will be spending most mornings rushing

around his boundaries dogging his birds back towards home. But with so much food on offer from a benevolent nature, the birds will often tend to wander no matter how good the feeding by the keeper. This can be make or break time for the shoot, with naive poults falling victim to cars, casual poachers, and a whole host of predators from foxes to mink and feral cats. Large kills are rare, but the continual loss of odd birds here and there can add up to a significant total if the keeper does not take care to keep his birds in safe places and control the worst predators.

For the pheasant keeper the first of October is the start of the shooting season, but it is rarely a date on which the Guns are out in force. A few early-hatched wild birds will be fully mature by this time, but the majority of pheasants will need another three or four weeks before they are really strong on the wing and able to provide testing sport.

There may, however, be earlier days for partridges, and increasing numbers of lowland shoots are now releasing a few redlegs to provide sport on these October days. Combined, perhaps, with a few wild greys which have been carefully nurtured, and even the odd wily old cock pheasant, these birds can provide superb sport on the warm days of autumn. They often move into the woods and cover crops later on too, so that the January days in the coverts include a few partridges.

For most lowland keepers however, October is the month of final preparations. They will be out with their boss selecting the places for the pegs on each drive, carefully calculating how to get the very best sport from the birds. Many drives will have two or more lines of pegs anyway so that they can be driven in different ways according to the weather on the day.

At the same time there may well be a briefing meeting with a few key beaters, to make sure that everyone knows how each drive is expected to unfold. The keeper knows that game shooting brings enormous pleasure, and that it is intended to be a combination of good fun and high excitement. If his planning and organisation is top notch, the shooting day will run with

**The keeper catches up his birds at the end of the season and pens them in an
aviary prior to their egg laying from which next year's shooting will come.
Good, young cock birds are preferred, one cock to eight or ten hens being the
norm**

relaxed efficiency. There will be no need for shouted orders, or irritated voices, as everyone knows what they are trying to achieve. The end result is that there is time for a little humour and banter, for game shooting brings with it a camaraderie which is rarely seen in any other walk of life.

Sadly, October has one other serious problem: it is when poaching becomes far more intensive: game prices are high because few birds are being shot, but at the same time the coverts are full, so poaching is comparatively easy. Given that most poachers operate under cover of darkness, the keeper is forced into a succession of sleepless nights all spent on watch. Since the poachers do not bother to ring him and say when they are coming, he has to be ever vigilant. Modern alarm equipment has helped, and it is now possible to set up devices which detect intruders without alerting them. Also, image-intensifying equipment can be a great boon, and can justify its expense. However, there is still no substitute for being on watch if you wish to stand a real chance of catching the poachers. This work is surely the unfairest cut of the whole keepering job, and it imposes severe strain on both the keeper and his family; but it must be done if the poachers are not to decimate the shooting.

And so at last, on some crisp November morn, it all comes together. Some early beaters will be out on stop duty in strategic places as Guns, beaters and pickers-up assemble in the shoot yard. Dogs bounce enthusiastically at their masters' heels, and people who have not seen each other for nine months exchange happy greetings in anticipation of three months of fine sport to come.

Eventually, all move off to the first covert; the Guns take their places, the horn blows, and beaters move quietly into the wood. After a few moments of sticks tapping, a spaniel punches into a bush and out rockets a fine cock pheasant, climbing hard and heading forward. In the gun line there is intense anticipation: everyone prays that the bird will go over his neighbour, for it is high and fast, and he does not want to be the one who missed the first bird of the season!

Later, as the season progresses, the birds get wilder and wilier, and the keeper decides on a change of plan. Too many birds have been slipping back out of the 'High Wood' drive, and so it is time to turn the tables on them, and drive them in the opposite direction. Given the right wind he knows that they will fly like dingbats in this reversed drive, to give a new pleasure to the Guns.

And so, as Christmas passes into January and we come full circle, the keeper's thoughts already begin to turn to next season. There is probably a breeding stock of hens to catch up before the season closes. More importantly, how can things be improved for next year? They did not really go so well from 'Marsh Covert', and 'The Beeches' never held the birds he had hoped for. Time to start reflecting on the season's results, and plan new

Catching up the hen pheasants at the end of the season is an important job:
should it fail, eggs will be in short supply and the rearing programme reduced.
The birds walk into traps set in the rides, and emptied at regular intervals

ways to improve coverts, and open the flushing rides on several drives. And so, even before the last shoot of the season is over, ideas are being worked on for the following year.

At the same time, it is now the season to thank the beaters and pickers-up. They will be invited to bring their own guns for a last January day, when cocks only will be the rule and there will be a reversal of roles with the Guns turning out to beat! This might be followed by February pigeon shoots when Guns and beaters alike enjoy fine sport together at the roosting pigeon, as these come to the woods after their days raiding the farmers' crops.

There may be a little cash for the helpers on shoot days, but that is not what they really care for. These people come for the love of the sport, and the camaraderie, and the fact that they feel a part of the place. The cock day and those February pigeon shoots which the keeper is able to give them, simply seal the bargain and provide the icing on the cake.

10
The Beater and his Dog

No driven shoot can operate without beaters, or 'brushers' as we call them in East Anglia. These good folk tramp weary miles and come whacking through the bushes to drive the game forwards, over the Guns, and thus provide them with sport. The walked-up bird, shot from behind is all very well and can be hard to hit, but the purist wants a driven bird, preferably as difficult a one as possible, and this is where the beater's role is so important.

Beating is a pleasant enough job and it allows many people to become involved in the sport who might otherwise not have the opportunity. The shooting field is a place of teamwork with many elements, each playing a part vital to the whole; leave one out and the operation fails, and the beater is one of the most important cogs in the shooting machine. I recommend the activity to husbands, wives, friends, children, girlfriends—anyone connected with the Guns who would like a day out, possibly a free lunch and maybe a tenner in their pocket at the end of it. They will be privileged to walk through private and preserved ground, they will be directly involved in a sporting event, and will have the opportunity to share the tactics and occasionally watch the shooting.

Once you have become a beater on a shoot and have proved your worth, the keeper will undoubtedly invite you again and you will find yourself a regular member of his squad, a position which many might envy you. In time you might run to buying and training a beating dog such as a spaniel, and in doing so you will commit yourself even more fully. In time you will learn your way about the shoot and thus enter more thoroughly into the spirit of the day, and will be able to make an even more effective contribution. You will learn the favourite escape routes of the birds, discover the places they tend to gather prior to flushing, and know which Guns on which pegs to watch.

It is important that a beater is well clothed as he or she is out in all weathers, struggling through dense cover or tramping across open fields with no protection from the driving rain. If you are cold or wet there is no fun in it and you are supposed to be enjoying yourself. Good, well fitting boots are essential: Wellingtons are standard wear in all but the driest of weathers, except on the grouse moor when leather boots are sometimes preferred for their better ankle support and grip on uneven ground, and the fact that feet tend to sweat less in them. Wellies and stout socks will serve on most occasions, but new boots of any sort should not be worn until they have been well broken in. A blister on a beater's foot is bad news.

Warm sweaters are advisable, although you will be exerting yourself for much of the time and it will not do to be too warm. Most important of all is the top coat and leggings. Traditionally these are of the waxproof sort made

Transport for the beaters is an important feature. Their comfort and safety
must be paramount and the legal requirements of such transport adhered to.
This trailer is not ideal, there being no back support for the passengers, no
step up for the aged and no cover in case of wind or rain

by Barbour which resist thorns and even barbed wire and keep the rain at bay. The trouble with waxproof is that the wearer tends to sweat as the cloth does not breathe. In Chapter 4 some of the new breathing fabrics for outdoor coats are described: some are expensive, more so than waxproof, but they do solve this particular problem. However, it is debatable whether they are robust enough for bursting through a quickthorn hedge or working out the middle of dense brambles; probably such a coat is too good for such treatment, so the waxproof topcoat remains, on balance, the best.

Leggings or overtrousers of the same material are standard wear for much the same reasons. Walking in wet kale or even long grass, quite apart from the prickly places, is hard on the lower leg and so stud-on leggings are favourite; fewer beaters tending to use the full trousers as these pull down off the waist as you walk and are hotter. A hat is essential to top off the ensemble, also gloves or handwarmers as required, and scarf ditto; put a bag of mints in your pocket and you are ready for anything. Most important of all is a good stick for bashing the bushes. This should not be your Sunday stick with the beautifully carved staghorn handle, but a stout ground ash or blackthorn one which you don't mind damaging.

The keeper or head beater is the guv'nor as far as you are concerned: what he says goes, and you must listen carefully to the instructions. It needs only one beater to misunderstand and do the wrong thing and a whole drive might be spoiled. A friend beating on a grey partridge shoot in Norfolk had been told by the keeper on no account to shout or make any noise, as the

birds were in a touchy mood. Crossing a ditch halfway through the drive my friend saw a good covey on the stubble before him. Forgetting the rules he bellowed enthusiastically and waved his stick aloft to send the birds the right way. The whole field erupted, with about 300 birds all taking off and flying away together. There was a spatter of shots as the Guns found themselves with a sudden cloud of shootable birds about their ears, and then it was all over. He was not invited to beat again.

The rules are fairly simple: the head beater places himself in the middle of the line, and everyone else keeps in line with him and covers the ground at the pace he sets, walking in the direction of the Guns. Variations and certain specialised tasks are possible, such as one beater being deputed to tap down a hedge which pheasants might use as an escape route; on a partridge or grouse shoot another might be entrusted with a flag to turn any birds which show a desire to slip out of the side of the drive. Usually these will be the more experienced members of the team.

Pheasants will hide in the densest part of the cover rather than fly, in the hope that the beaters will pass them by; later in the season they grow especially crafty and take some putting on the wing. It is not for the beater to skirt fastidiously round the side of the brambles, the dense bracken or stand of thorn: the good one is right in there, bashing about with his stick—standing by on the outside and tapping half-heartedly is not good enough and birds will remain unflushed. When a pheasant rises or a covey goes forward there is a temptation for the beater to stop tapping and watch to see if the bird is hit or missed as it passes the Guns.

Gentle tapping is one of the greatest weapons in the beater's armoury. It is this which moves the birds quietly forward to the flushing places—a sinister tap-tapping from a dozen or more stout-hearted beaters will move the game on steadily and without panic. The sound seems to vibrate through the ground, and without over-startling anything, just puts it afoot and keeps it moving—if you stop your tapping, especially in a field of roots, the birds will tend to come back between you. This is more likely the closer to the end of the drive that you are. Pheasants will want to run back then, but the deadly tapping stops them; respite gives them the chance they need. The rule is simple: watch the bird by all means, but *keep tapping*.

Keep a good line. It is easy to become preoccupied with your own affairs and with tapping here and there, and you might lose sight of the other beaters in woodland or behind a hedge. So keep an eye on the rest, glancing regularly from right to left, and keep in line—if you are miles ahead or miles behind you make a gap in the line through which the birds will not just leak, they will pour. So much of any country sport is about looking and listening while remaining unobtrusive, and it applies as much to beating as to anything.

There is no need to shout. There is always an urge to give vent to a primitive war whoop when a bird gets up and flies forward, but the Guns will have seen it, thank you very much, so your bellowing is superfluous. The best teams of beaters are identified by—among other things—the absence of Red Indian war cries as they approach. It is hard, especially when young, to curb natural, noisy exuberance, but it goes down badly both with

Labrador

Springer

Flatcoat

Pointer

Guns and some keepers; besides the beater is a member of a team and is being paid to do a job to the specification of the employer—shouting adds nothing to his effectiveness, and indeed can be counter-productive, as we have seen.

Keep an eye on the others in the team and learn from them—though some of the most seasoned old-timers are not necessarily good models. No point in growing old unless you also grow crafty, and some senior beaters have made a fine art of skirting the rough places, leaving such for the wives and youngsters while they themselves stroll along the stubble. I have seen this often, and a good keeper or shoot captain will make sure that their days on the estate are numbered. Others will be working hard to provide sport— nothing is too much trouble, they volunteer for the extra walk, use their initiative, and go through and not round the impenetrable cover; moreover they appear to be enjoying themselves, are quiet and watchful, and understand the complexities of driven shooting.

Many shooting folk turn to beating or picking-up if they abandon their gun in later years, or when they feel like a change. They realise how much they would miss the interest, the fresh air and exercise, and the involvement in such a privileged occasion as well as the challenge which it can be, and this is one way they can still play an active role in the sport.

The Beater's Dog

Time was when the beater was discouraged from bringing a dog, and as a rule, no dogs were allowed in the beating line. The standards of training were, I suspect, not as good forty years ago as they are today, and few dogs could be trusted not to run wild if left to their own devices. In open woodland a dog is largely superfluous, as also on stubbles where once the partridges lay in covey after covey which flushed easily enough. Another argument I have heard against the beating dog is that a team of good dogs can be too efficient, sweeping all the game forward at the risk of too great a slaughter, with not sufficient stock spared to lead the survivors back to cover at the end of the day.

Times have changed and good dogs—with an emphasis on the good—are welcome in the beating line. A beater with a dog is a more effective contributor and adds another dimension to the day's sport. The beater's dog is a hunter rather than a retriever, its job being to quarter the ground from side to side and back and forth, never wandering more than about 20 metres away but working thoroughly, flushing the game and pushing it in the direction of the Guns. The human beater uses his eyes, the canine one its nose: this means that the pheasant tucked in under the brambles, the one deep in the furze or so far down in the tangle of old rushes that it has a job to extricate itself, will no longer be passed by.

A man with a dog does the work of three good beaters, although this is no reason for the dog man to assume delusions of grandeur, for the human beater has a vital role. However, a dog does justify the pound or two extra which traditionally is paid to its handler and another benefit from the

keeper's point of view, is that a dog in the line will often retrieve birds lost from previous drives, dead ones which no-one suspected were there, or runners which had eluded the pickers-up. It is not unusual for beaters with dogs to retrieve a handful of pheasants as they make their way through a drive. The drawback to this is that the beating dog learns to peg birds rather than make them run forwards—but you cannot have everything.

Like all dogs, the beating dog works better into the wind. If the drive happens to run downwind he may well run well forward towards the Guns and then work back, flushing birds towards the beaters. Another risk is that the dog works beyond the control of the handler and makes multiple flushes which are a horror to the keeper and the shoot captain, while the dog owner wishes the ground would swallow him up. Furthermore, the dog should work in silence; a yapping spaniel tearing about after rabbits or running pheasants in a wood does not bring out the best in even the most gentle and friendly keeper.

The dog should work to command, flushing steadily and under control,

never giving tongue, covering the ground, and working to the whistle rather than the human voice. A lot of shouting directed at dogs working in cover spoils the effect of a beating line and the Guns do not like it. Also be warned that even if the dog is willing, able and positively encouraged to retrieve runners from the previous drive, it should *not* leave the cover at the conclusion of a drive, run forward and retrieve shot birds lying in the open on the stubble. This happens more often than you might think, the dog picking up one bird and taking it back to its master, or worse, picking one and dropping it in favour of another, or even engaging in a tug o' war with a Gun's dog for the same bird; such behaviour causes annoyance all round. The picker-up and Gun who shot the birds do not know where they are then, and such a dog should not be permitted to work with the beaters.

The dog for beating should be a hunting dog, and I have mentioned the English springer spaniel as one of the favourites: it is good in cover, works the ground thoroughly, is a good retriever, companion, handy in water, unafraid of the rough stuff and easily available. However, when you have bought and trained your first dog and won permission to bring it in the beating line, you will discover that some keepers show a curious lack of understanding of working dogs and what they can achieve. Take this fictitious example: as dogger you are instructed to work your way through an impenetrable patch of cover while everyone else is in fairly open country; you are told to 'bring it through—nice and steadily', so you set off into an acre of rhododendrons, with the dog going on ahead. However, the crashing of the foliage in its ears makes it deaf to any whistle, the handler has to struggle to keep upright, with visibility of only a few feet—and yet is expected to keep control of the dog and flush every pheasant in the cover.

Meanwhile the rest of the line is marching on boldly, the other beaters and keeper taking it all far too fast for you in your little piece of jungle and certainly too quickly for your dog to do an efficient job, even assuming he is still in the same county as you. The most versatile and adaptable dog would find such an ordeal difficult.

You only have to look at any good beating dog at the end of the day to know just how much heart and effort it has to put into its work: it is likely to be completely exhausted, wet and shivering. The beater must towel down his animal and give it a feed, then bed it down in comfort in his vehicle and get it home as soon as possible.

On open moorland or over big country such as the root fields and stubbles of East Anglia, one of the Hunter Pointer Retriever breeds will serve well as a beating dog.

No shoot could operate without a good team of beaters: besides, there are worse ways of passing a Saturday afternoon.

The English springer spaniel is one of the most popular, all-purpose gundogs, more often seen in the beating line than in the company of a standing gun. Full of bounding enthusiasm and bustle, no shooting field would be complete without at least one of them

11
The Picker-Up

No formal driven shoot worth its name, however small, should operate without at least one picker-up. His job is to retrieve wounded game which has passed over and far behind the Guns, birds which have received a pellet or two and which to all intents and purposes are lost to them and too time-consuming for them to go and hunt out. The picker-up is therefore positioned far back where such birds are likely to plane down, where, operating independently from the rest of the field, he can devote time to recovering them. His role is one of common humanity, for a countryside littered with wounded game is not a scenario any sportsman would care to have on his conscience.

If a picker-up gathers just one wounded bird in a day, a bird which otherwise would have been lost, then duty is done and honour satisfied. It stands to reason that while a small shoot with modest bags might be able to manage with just one or two PUs, the large shoot will need as many as one per Gun, for once a PU has committed himself to finding one bird, others might be planing down unmarked by him. (I say 'him' but a great many of the best pickers-up I know happen to be ladies.)

For a shoot to skimp on PUs is short-sighted, bad policy and, I would go as far as to say, bad sportsmanship: any game deserves better than to be left, wounded and suffering, for the sake of the modest fee a PU commands. Like the beater, the PU is not there to make a living, but because he enjoys working his dogs and sharing in a sporting occasion. If the money pays his petrol and buys a pint that night he is more than satisfied. Some will come purely for the love of it.

Even more than the beater, the PU needs to learn the layout of the shoot. Newcomers are welcome provided they can be overseen by those more experienced, and as long as their dogs are of proven ability; but the experienced PU knows the places where wounded birds are likely to be found, he is familiar with the short-cuts about the estate, is unlikely to get lost and understands the tactics of the various drives. The dogs of the regulars soon become match fit, and quickly learn the evasive ways of game, the handler likewise! Any dog will do provided it is soft-mouthed, and a hard worker with a good nose and not afraid of rough cover. The two most popular breeds are the springer spaniel and the labrador, with a leaning towards the latter.

A good picker-up, dressed demurely but practically, is seen little if at all on a shooting day. The odd glimpse on the far side of forty acres of heavy plough is the best you can hope for. If he or she retrieves just one bird which would otherwise be lost the wages are justified. Many will retrieve a great many more

Like the rest of the team, the PU should be willing and enthusiastic. One of the drawbacks of knowing a shoot *too* well is that the old vitality can begin to wane. There might be a temptation to take short-cuts, the edge you get when working a new place grows stale until, without really noticing it, you find you are not trying as hard as you did. If you have not already been invited by an observant shoot captain or keeper to seek pastures new, you should make the decision for yourself, or at least take a break from picking up for a few weeks.

The task of picking up has another side: on a commercial shoot where the bag is expected to be large, the picker-up may also act as a 'hoover', gathering the birds shot which are lying dead nearby. On such a day you will be one of a team, with others much further back collecting the runners, droppers and pricked birds. The bottom line is that you are to collect *all* game, but as with most rules, there are exceptions: the main one is when the Guns have dogs of their own. While they will have neither time nor inclination to go right to the back of the wood to seek a lightly pricked bird, they do like to try their dogs on easy ones lying nearby.

It is therefore not fair to them for the picker-up to flash about showing off his field trial dog and snatching birds from under their noses. Besides, picking up birds lying dead on grass or short stubble and so easy that a child of five could retrieve them, is hardly a challenge and least of all for the professional PU; so to see him staggering back to the game cart with armfuls of dead birds collected from within fifty yards is not impressive. What is he being paid for?

You should go for everything the keeper asks: he does not warm to the argument that such a retrieve in those particular circumstances might ruin your dog and upset its carefully regulated training. He wants the birds in the bag.

At the start of the drive you ought to be in position at least a hundred metres behind the Guns; do not hide in the ditch bottom, but be conspicuous: stand out a few paces from the wood or hedgerow the better to get a view of where birds are going in—if you stay in the thick you can see only a few yards in each direction. If you are limited by the farm boundary, a road or a railway and have to stand closer to the Guns, then the reason to be conspicuous is even more sound. It is the PUs who hide behind bushes who are shot by careless Guns, or Guns who were not aware that they were there. A good Gun will look round to see where you are, and a good host or shoot captain will have made it clear that you are thereabouts.

You ought to have your own transport. Sometimes it is important for you to wait behind after the drive to work on an especially tricky runner and the whole field must not be kept waiting; the keeper has a set number of drives, and while he must honour the commitment to seek and find lost game, these drives must nonetheless be covered. You will find several birds which the Guns believed they had missed; a surprising number of birds are struck by a single pellet and will fall dead far behind, having given no sign of being hit. This is especially true of pheasants.

The PU will usually find these lying dead, and he ought to let the Gun

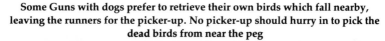

Some Guns with dogs prefer to retrieve their own birds which fall nearby, leaving the runners for the picker-up. No picker-up should hurry in to pick the dead birds from near the peg

know that a bird has been retrieved. This is very encouraging to a Gun, as it is when a picker-up finds a bird which the Gun has especially pointed out to him. To seek out that Gun a couple of hours later and say 'I found that cock from the second drive; it came down in the brambles at the back of the wood', is to give the Gun a genuinely warm glow which survives several subsequent misses. Another tip is to hunt round the pegs of Guns after they have gone. A noted Cambridgeshire picker-up, Robin Wise, holds the theory that most Guns can only count up to three, after which they become hazy. Dead game is often left lying in the open round the pegs, having been overlooked by everyone.

If you are regular on the shoot you will soon learn that the information you get from some Guns needs careful analysis. There are some who—not to put too fine a point upon it—claim hard hits for birds which they have not even touched. You can waste an awful lot of time slogging about on the far side of a field of heavy plough looking for birds which everyone knows are not there.

There are various ruses to deal with this; one is the PU who secretes a bird or two about his person and emerges from behind the bushes where he has been having a quiet smoke and announces that he has found it. However, this might encourage the Gun and make him worse; it also gets the PU into bad habits. A certain giveaway that a PU is trying this dodge is when he inquires, 'Cock or hen, sir?', as he sets off—as if that mattered. He just wants to bring back a bird of the same sex as the one the Gun claims is breathing its last, a quarter of a mile away in the brambles.

Alternatively you can try for it but return quickly, or maybe just make the pretence of going—but with the risk that, like the little boy who cried 'Wolf!', the Gun one day just might be right. Honesty might be painful, but it is probably the best policy if you can carry it out without hurting the feelings of the Gun: he is there to enjoy himself, remember, and you are paid to help him do so.

There is a sub-species of the same breed which claims to have 'certainly hit the bird, but not very hard'. His usual cry is 'Sure to be a dead bird by now', or 'It won't have gone far'; both claims proved wrong so often as to be past debate.

The good Guns and the ones you come to trust are those who can give you a precise location of every dead and wounded bird they have shot during the drive. The ability to do this comes with experience—and if they have shot nothing, they will say so, and not waste your time. What you do *not* want, as a PU, is an airy wave of the hand in the general direction of a faraway block of woodland. A good Gun watches his birds down in case the PU has missed them, and can tell to within a yard where they pitched in, how hard they were hit and also what their likely course of action will be.

The picker-up should be dressed much as the beaters, with clothing which resists the weather and is proof against thorns and dense cover. A shooting stick is handy to take the weight during the drive, and some people favour a compact pair of binoculars, useful for watching a towering bird which fades into the distance. A thumbstick is useful and you will have with you your usual doggy paraphernalia of whistle, leads and so on. Like the beater's dog,

Pheasant crossing right to left; easy to miss for the right-hander

Left: The peg dog must stay with its master during the drive

Top: A right-and-left at woodcock is a dream for most shooting folk

Above: All shot game must be hung up as soon as possible

An open ride gives the beaters a chance to straighten the line

that of the PU also needs special attention after a hard day's work: a handful of biscuit and a good towelling down, plus a comfortable dry place in the vehicle are vital.

There are mixed views about the carrying of a 'priest', or game dispatcher. The very nature of your work means that some birds will come to hand which are not dead, and part of your expertise lies in being able to dispatch these without fuss so as to minimise their suffering. It ought to be possible for you to develop the professional skill to wring a bird's neck or, more properly, to break it neatly without having to resort to bashing with a priest (so called, incidentally, because it is a priest who administers the last rites). The best alternative is one of the pliers-type of humane game dispatchers of the Semark-BASC or Shooting Developments sort, which work well for all winged game from a snipe to a goose.

Another debatable point concerns game bags: some PUs are in favour of them, others not. To have a brace of birds encumbering your hands as you hunt for a third is a nuisance, so clearly you need something. The over-the-shoulder game carrier is a good compromise—it folds up when not in use, but is capable of carrying about six brace of pheasants—probably more weight than you would care to carry far!

Upmarket shoots operate a system of walkie-talkies to enable shoot

Overleaf
It is a great help if the pickers-up have their own transport in order to be independent of the rest of the shooting field. The picker-up must be able to devote as much time as is necessary to making difficult and lengthy retrieves: this vital operation is not one to be hurried

captain, keeper, head beater and pickers-up to be in easy contact. This system has its points, but it can be cumbersome; also much airwave space is wasted in needless directions, and many shoots operate perfectly well without it. If you find this is the custom of the shoot then you must make the best of it.

The PU must be careful not to disturb ground which is to be driven later, and not to continue his activity in roosting cover at a time when pheasants are drawing in for the night. The time and disturbance involved in hunting out one bird must be set against the importance of allowing the resident game to go up to roost, and of not causing it, by your presence, to wander off possibly over the boundary.

My own view of the picker-up is that the best are those you never see: you might catch a glimpse of one standing watchfully far back at the start of the drive, but thereafter a little van creeping along a ride or a shadowy figure lurking with dogs far off in the scrub is all the Gun ought to see. At the end of the day when all are gathered together discussing the sport, the little van will appear and the picker-up emerge with a couple of handfuls of birds which otherwise would have been lost. Such a person is worth ten times what you pay them—but luckily for us, they all love the sport and working their dogs.

12
Mixed Bag

Just Laws to Make Just Men

The shooting world is a mass of written rules as well as the unwritten ones as examined in Chapter 7. Ignorance of the law is no excuse for transgression, and it is vital that the shooter is familiar with those which affect him and his sport. A booklet published by HMSO and entitled *Shotguns: A Guide to the Law* sets out the basis of the rules, which have recently been amended (1989) in the light of public outcry after the disaster of Hungerford. The booklet explains only the basis of the rules; for the finer points, the whole Firearms Amendment Act should be studied.

A shotgun has a barrel length not less than 24in and a bore of 2in or less in diameter. Either it has no magazine at all, or it has a hand-detachable one (such as on a bolt-action weapon), which cannot hold more than two cartridges and is not a revolver gun with a chamber which goes round when it is fired. To possess such a gun, a shotgun certificate has for long been necessary but since 1 July 1989 the issuing process has been considerably tightened up.

The new style certificate will contain details of all the guns held by the applicant, including their identification numbers if known. The new certificate specifies that the guns should be kept in a secure place, the precise nature of which is not defined but which by default and the interpretation of many chief constables, has come to mean some sort of steel cabinet with security locks.

Four photographs of the applicant must be submitted with each application, and the form countersigned by some pillar of the community who attests to the applicant's God-fearing and responsible character. The certificate runs for three years, although consideration is being given to extending that period to five years, thus reducing the bureaucracy.

The chief constable may not refuse your application provided it complies with the regulations, but he has the right to oppose it if he is not satisfied that you may possess a shotgun without danger to the public; or if he feels that you have no good reason for possessing a shotgun or if he believes that you have been prohibited from possessing one. Assuming you have no record of violent crime, of lunacy, mental instability or fits, there is no good reason why your application should be refused. Shooting game, vermin, clay targets or even keeping guns as part of a collection are all acceptable as good reasons for possession.

If the police refuse an application for any of the above reasons, the applicant has the right of appeal and it is by no means a foregone conclusion that the police will prevail. Test cases include the chief constable who used a conviction for driving with excess alcohol in the blood as a reason to withold

a certificate. There are some authorities where the police make no secret of the fact that they would like to reduce the number of shotgun owners to nil, and they go out of their way to be obstructive and difficult about all applications. At least one authority awards its officers 'Brownie points' if they return from a shotgun certificate application home visit having persuaded or brow-beaten the applicant into surrendering his rights to gun ownership.

A policeman may ask for your certificate at any time when you are in possession of your gun and out shooting, so it is wise to have the document with you. The paper is bulky and inconvenient to carry, and is designed to fit in no pocket known to any tailor. A photocopy of the front sheet might serve at a pinch, but there is no promise that this will be acceptable.

The certificate must be produced every time you purchase ammunition. This is not easy when you buy mail order, but special arrangements can be made.

If you buy or sell a shotgun, and assuming that both buyer and seller are holders of a shotgun certificate, the seller must transfer details of the gun onto the new holder's certificate. Within seven days of the transaction he must send notice of the event to the chief constable who issued his own certificate, and the buyer also must send notification of the transfer to the chief constable who issued *his* certificate. All details of the gun should be included, the make, model, distinguishing features and serial number. It is recommended that the letters containing this information ought to be sent by registered post or recorded delivery. It all sounds a great deal of fun to do, and ought to keep many good folk in employment sorting it all out.

The penalty for possession of a firearm without proper authority is six months imprisonment or a fine of £2,000. If you are a visitor to this country or are considering inviting a shooter from overseas you should obtain a copy of the leaflet *Gun Permits for Visitors to Great Britain*. Those under the age of fifteen may hold a shotgun certificate subject to the restrictions mentioned, but they may not carry or use it unless they are in the company of a certificate holder aged over twenty-one. Those from fifteen to seventeen may use a gun unsupervised but may not buy a gun or ammunition.

It is an offence to shoot on land where permission has not been granted. Every square inch of ground in the country belongs to someone, be it county council, the Crown or a landowner, and the shooting rights are either in hand or disposed of in some way. Free shooting is a thing of the past. The game shooter is unlikely to be troubled with boundaries as he will tend to go where he is sent. There are forbidden lines which it is possible to cross unless you have made sure first where they are. A bird dropping just over the fence ought to be retrieved but only after consultation with the host, and then only if you leave your gun on your own side. Most shoots operate a 'good neighbour' policy and reciprocal arrangements are made.

Transgression of the gun law today is a serious matter and it is easy to get it wrong. The awesome powers of the police to oppose and have a shotgun certificate withdrawn are sufficient reason to ensure that it never happens to you. Ignorance is no excuse. To aid and abet are also offences, so do not lend unauthorised guns. Leaving weapons in your house unsecured could result in your certificate being contested, as could your having them on display in an unlocked, or even a locked car, if your conduct could be deemed as irresponsible. Idleness or carelessness have caused many a gun to pass the night uncleaned leaning in a corner after a shooting day. The rules have changed, and with them must change the practices of the bad old days where weapons could be left out in barns for decades and be quite safe. The onus now is firmly on the shooting man to take care of dangerous weapons, and to convince the general public by his actions that the sporting Shot does not in any way constitute a risk to civil peace and quiet.

Big Bags

In Chapter 10 I indicated that some obscenely huge bags had been made in the days when the sport was still establishing itself, embroiled in growing pains. Estate vied with estate to produce the greatest mountain of the slain, though even then there was a criticism that quality was being sacrificed on the altar of quantity. The royal patronage and the First Eleven of great Shots were partly to blame for this greedy bag-filling, and thankfully World War I saw an end to it. The slaughter in the fields of France gave slaughter a bad taste even by the covert-sides of the great estates, and the big Shots went into hibernation.

There were those who never deserted the lunatic obsession for huge bags of poorish pheasants, but the majority settled down to smaller numbers of better quality. Man tends not to learn from his mistakes and the last two decades saw a return to the worst excesses of Edwardian game shooting: suddenly there was a generation of business folk and foreign visitors with money to spare. 'Hospitality days' boomed, and that peculiarly eighties phenomenon, the 'yuppie', suddenly had a yen to walk in the footsteps of the great Shots, to shoot the coverts of estates with legendary names in the hope that some of the old nobility would rub off. In most cases he knew little of shooting, of sportsmanship, marksmanship, or what went into producing a pheasant, let alone a pheasant shoot. For him the exercise was a social occasion, full stop: the lunch and dinner tended to be the most important parts.

Shoots tolerated this trend and, let it be said, encouraged it, on the grounds that the revenue kept many keepers in employment and saved the estates from being sold or broken up and the woods destroyed to make way for more profitable ventures. In my view this was a bad period in British game shooting: we had the potential and reputation for the best sport in the world and we made it into the worst simply because of greed.

The early 1990s saw new winds of change blowing through the pheasant woods. The first was a simple matter of economics. The 'yuppie' hospitality shooting market had been paying up to £20.00 per pheasant shot, and in the many cases where they could not hit them, the rate was changed to £20.00 per three cartridges fired, this being the only way the estate could make any money on a day of moderate Shots. The collapse of the economy killed the business overnight, the exploitive shoots going to the wall and the rest reducing their rearing programmes and re-learning some valuable lessons.

The receding wave left behind it those who could still afford the best, and those from overseas to shoot the finest grouse and top quality pheasants, together with others who did not want huge bags but would pay for quality birds in smaller numbers. Half-tame things which flopped reluctantly out of the tops of oak plantings and flapped by, were no longer considered the epitomy of the good shoot. A handful of high-flying, testing birds was the thing, and not a mountain of pathetic, half-feathered poults at the end of the day. The decline in the market for dead game hastened the change, as many recognised the bad publicity resulting from shooting birds which no-one would ever eat and which they were forced through lack of a market to bury. Such a practice undermined the basic philosophy of all field shooting sports, namely that everything you shoot is eaten, if not by you, then by someone else.

A further evolutionary step was quietly gathering momentum, and this was the phenomenon of the do-it-yourself game shoot. This was a move away from the rigid formality of the cover shoot run in the old ways by the old people, towards a system where a team of enthusiasts rented and improved their own ground, carrying out rearing and vermin control, and organising the whole shoot themselves in their spare time. They would have no keeper as such but might employ someone part-time to feed or trap. If possible the landowner would be persuaded to join them and spinneys could be planted, cover crops set, and in time, previously unshot land developed to show good potential.

Such a shoot is run for the members and their personal guests and with no commercial pressures, devoted to the showing of fewer, quality birds, for those who shot down poor ones early in the year are only detracting from their own sport later in the season. Such shoots can be run on a financial shoe-string, the rent of the land being the largest outgoing, the rearing of game birds the next. Thanks to the research of the Game Conservancy, the methodology of habitat improvement, feeding and vermin control has been brought within the reach of the DIY shooting man so that the necessity for rearing is reduced to a minimum.

On natural game-holding land such as East Anglia or Hampshire, wild stocks may be increased to a level where they alone will provide good sport. It is important in such cases that the shoot captain has a good knowledge of his game population, of what he needs to leave for next year and what he can afford to shoot. The shootable surplus will depend in part on his efficiency as a game holder, feeder and controller of vermin, but mainly on the weather— a foul breeding season will reduce the success rate of hatching and thus his shootable surplus. Teams of Guns shooting the DIY shoot need to be understanding enough to exercise restraint when called upon: in a really bad pheasant year they may have to make do with cocks only.

The general message is that we must be happy to shoot fewer birds, but look for better quality. Discernment and discretion are important elements in the make-up of the shooting man, and those who rush into amassing greedy bags of poor birds are fewer and are beginning to be frowned upon by the shooting community at large. The number shot in a day is no longer of any great importance—some shoots can take large rearing programmes and have the ground and keepering strength to do it, so it would be a mistake to mention a magic, optimum figure—but what is all-important now is that they should be good, well shown birds. A sportsman will allow the poor stuff to pass him by, and take the bird which represents a challenge and has a sporting chance of getting away . . .

Public opinion is a new factor, and it is partly to counter pressures from that quarter that some of our national bodies exist. The modern country dweller tends to have urban roots. He may live in the hamlet, but to him rural life is the picture seen on a calendar: there is no cow dung in the road, crowing cockerels, nasty smells or loud bangs from the stubble down the lane. His concept of a chicken is a frozen thing in a polythene bag from the supermarket. The true countryman knows that everything has a season; the farmers who compiled the Book of Ecclesiastes knew it too. We plant, sow, reap, live, die, rear up and cut down according to the ancient rhythm of the country year; it has always been so.

The public have been weaned away from such matters and find it hard to reconcile the sportsman taking life in what seems to them to be a needless manner and because, as they imagine, he revels in bloodshed and is gratuitously cruel. The sportsman is following traditional rural pastimes, and it is his interest that ensures that stocks of his game are available and protected, and that their habitat is enhanced, which in turn benefits all manner of secondary eco systems; also what he shoots is eaten, and more important, is *surplus* to what is required to guarantee next year's stock. He takes a harvest from the land as much as the farmer with his scythe or the

For a lad to shoot his first of anything is a momentous event, but a grouse might be the most triumphant moment of all. Young Duncan Clarke shot his first bird on a Yorkshire grouse moor which his late father Michael Clarke had made his own, so this was a doubly poignant moment

fisherman with his nets.

It all takes a while to explain, and there seems no time these days to convince the unconvincable; and we must accept that there is a large army of those living in both town and country to whom field sports are unintelligible. Nevertheless, the game Shot must be seen to be approachable, prepared to defend his activities when called on, and he must take the fight to the opposition by talking to youngsters, involving friends in beating on shoots, making presents of game and so on. The shooting man must be good at PR.

The rough shooter comes and goes walking up his pheasants, wildfowling or pigeon decoying with few any the wiser. The full-blown game shoot has a higher profile, easier for the 'antis' to disrupt, and more conspicuous in every way.

Guests

The regimen of the formal game shoot does not lend itself to the bringing of guests unless permission has been sought in advance. Even a chum to stand behind you, carry the gun, spectate and just be a companion breaks the rules of hospitality. The host will have done his catering for food and transport. A gaggle of wives and girlfriends, uninvited and tagging along, is annoying for the host and plain bad manners. It is not unusual to see a non-shooting friend on a shooting day, but there by arrangement; you would not bring a chum uninvited to a house party, and the same is the case in the formal shooting field. No problem if you ask, as long as you do not mind a straight answer; and even so, I think you would need to know your host very well before you posed the question. Asking if your son/daughter/friend might come and help swell the beating line is a good a start as any.

My wife once came as an invited guest on a shoot in the village next door. I deputed to her the task of hanging on to my dog name Kenzie who was something of a handful. Halfway through one drive a hen pheasant came straight at me from in front, one of the easiest shots. I blotted it out with the muzzles, flipped through and fired. The bird folded dead in the air and came hurtling down straight at me. Nimbly I stepped aside and the missile struck the memsahib fair and square between the shoulder blades and sent her flying.

She suffered fearful bruising and it was a week before the pain had gone. A falling game bird is no mean projectile—a mass weighing up to 4lb for a cock pheasant and flying at, say, 40mph can deal a serious blow. Over the years a number of Guns shooting in grouse butts have been stunned by falling grouse, which are less than 1lb in weight; a wild goose falling in the same way would flatten you. A guest or loader standing with you at your peg and who, unlike the Gun, might not be watching every bird that falls, is at a certain risk of being struck by falling game. It is a point worth making.

The shooting field is a place to remain alert, both to savour the event in its rich complexity and to ensure your own safety.

Some time before the shoot the keeper will put out the pegs at which the Guns
are to stand. Shoots number from either direction, depending on local custom,
but the keeper sets his pegs to give every position the chance of some shooting
and make sure that no one finds himself directly behind a tall tree

Changing Times

Time was when rabbit shooting was an entertaining side-line for the great
game Shots. Rabbits would be kept in warrens with a warrener paid to look
after them, a commercial enterprise, for rabbits were a source of food and the
shrewd owner of the warren improved on his income by letting the shooting
to the gentry on condition that he could keep the dead rabbits.

The Guns stood forward and the coneys were driven towards them. The
bags were stupendous, sometimes running into well over a thousand in a
day when the smoke of the black powder from innumerable cartridges hung
heavy in the dells. Also featured were a great many shooting mishaps, for

ground game is a notorious causer of accidents and many pepperings of ankles and legs, not to mention dogs. On one such shoot in 1887 every single beater was hit. In those days being shot by a member of the aristocracy was deemed a compliment and excellent jest combined. One noble Duke, when informed that he had shot a boy, said 'A what?'; 'A boy, your Grace'. 'Well, tell him not to let me catch him out again today'. Another noble Gun faced the beaters as the rabbits streamed through and bellowed 'Straddle your legs, man, and I'll shoot them as they run between'.

The driven rabbit is a thing of the past, and the only rabbiting with a gun that the modern, complete game Shot might expect is over ferrets or terriers, more a sport for the rough shooter than the covert-side beau. The only relic of those days is the rule in force on many game shoots 'Take nothing on the ground'.

Poachers

The arts of the poacher are as old as the biblical 'snare of the fowler'. Dealing with this pest is a job not for the complete game Shot but for the keeper and his allies. It is proper, however, that all should be aware of this menace which affects the countryside. Poaching a century ago was a matter of the poor man taking what he could to feed his family in times of hardship and cruel Victorian Game Laws; he ran enormous risks and at one time could easily have been maimed by spring gun or man trap. If caught he faced eviction for his family and deportation for himself. Others did 'a bit o' night work' for pure devilment and because the urge was strong.

Much has changed. The traditional need to poach is no longer there for no-one is starving; the Draconian Game Laws have been repealed and nobody risks facing a life-term in Van Dieman's land for taking a pheasant. Some poachers retain the ancient urge and some just cannot resist a bird for the pot, and few keepers would lose much sleep over the likes of them. Quite a different matter is the other trend, where well armed gangs of violent and ruthless men mark an estate and come on a likely night, mob-handed, and clear a man's coverts. We have seen how much work the keeper puts into producing birds for your sport and this way of robbing him of the fruits of his hard work, and selling it for beer money at the back door of pubs and hotels, is shameful.

The modern operator does not deserve the name of poacher; which truly belongs to those old-timers who knew the woods and fields, and the habits of the game that lived there, as well as, and often better than the keeper himself. The modern version is no more than a glorified burglar, crude in method and ignorant of the ways of the countryside, stealing the fruits of another man's labour and violent if cornered. Game prices have been low so the incentive to poach should have been reduced, and yet the grisly 'game' still goes on.

The most common method used by today's poacher is to stalk about the coverts at night with a silenced .22 rifle, air rifle or silenced .410. The

175

pheasants roost in the trees and low bushes, being especially fond of thorns, where they are conspicuously silhouetted against the night sky. On a stormy night the birds will sit tight and not take flight so unscrupulous poachers can shoot down a great number of them—the cunning ones enter a wood and work through it, noting the positions of the birds in the trees. At the furthest point they retrace their steps, shooting as they go, so that they are making their way homewards. The silenced weapon makes little noise, especially on a stormy night, and the only sign next day that a keeper has been 'done' is a markedly reduced number of birds on the feed ride, and the tell-tale star-shaped splashes of feathers under the trees showing where a bird hit the ground.

Sometimes the fields are combed with a trail net: this is swept back and forth between two men and takes the pheasants and partridges which have roosted on the ground in the stubble or among the sugarbeet leaves. It was an old method used most widely in the eastern counties, and it is still tried occasionally—and very deadly it can be. The keeper who suspects his fields are vulnerable to a local netting gang need do no more than scatter a few thorn bushes about. These will become entangled in the net and put an end to operations.

Another annoyance to the shooting man, sporting tenant or landowner is illegal hare coursing. This is often carried out by travelling folk who don't actually want the hares, for which they have no particular use, but who are keen to try their dogs against them. Great sums of money change hands in bets, and for selling and buying the greyhounds. These folk can be threatening and are hard to bring to book, some police authorities freely admitting that they cannot be bothered with the problem. The annoyance is the disturbance caused to game coverts, and it is also the principle, that someone is on your land and you seem unable to do a thing about it.

The modern keeper will guard his coverts at night, equipped with two-way radio and car-phone to summon the police if needed. He is a brave man if he tackles the thugs single-handed, and is wiser not to do so.

The gamekeeper is an often misunderstood figure, and his ranks are on the decline, two reasons being the expense of running a game shoot and the rise of the DIY set-up. I have already cited the hostile attitude of the lay

public to country sports, and the keeper has this brought home to him by those who wander freely through his coverts at sensitive times of year, and generally make his life difficult. In the bad old days the woods were strictly preserved, for the trampling feet of the masses have a habit of destroying that which they come to see. Nowadays, the mobility bestowed by the motor car, the drift to the rural countryside, and a general interest in conservation issues have brought the urban public out and about.

The keeper must be a good PR man, willing and able to talk to youngsters at the local school and dispel the traditional image of 'gruff old velveteens'. Trouble arises when the keeper finds his traps broken or thrown away; but the control—*not* the elimination—of ground and winged vermin is essential in the modern, managed countryside; other creatures benefit by a reduction of their enemies at breeding time. The countryside we so admire is the one created by the sporting farmer and his gamekeeper 150 years ago. The vandal will be always with us, but his arrival at the covert-side goes to support the view that the lot of the modern keeper, hemmed in as he is by legislation and constraints, is not an easy one.

13
From Field to Table

by Angela Humphreys

After the many weeks of tender loving care that go into producing a memorable day's shooting, it is fitting that the bag should be treated with the respect it deserves. When the gamekeeper presents you with a hand-picked brace of birds at the end of the day, it is your responsibility to see that they are equally lovingly prepared for the table.

The Hanging Debate

During a well organised shoot, birds will be hung for transit in the open air or in the game cart, and will not be tightly packed into a game bag and left all day. Game should be removed from the car as soon as you arrive home, and *not* left under a pile of coats and wellies to be sorted out next day!

Fortunately there are no written rules about how long to hang game before it is cooked, as this depends on its condition, personal preference and, of course, the weather. Hang birds by the neck, and hares by their feet in a cool

As with all shot game, the quicker it arrives at the larder the better. Birds should be hung singly or by the brace in a cool, airy place, out of the reach of dogs and cats. The hanging of game is a matter under scrutiny by the EC. Only hung game develops the rich, 'gamey' flavour so appreciated by gourmets

airy place. Use a game larder, or drape with muslin if there are likely to be flies around. In warm humid weather game may only need to hang for two to three days; in colder conditions a fortnight may not be too long. If the flesh between the legs and breast is still white it is not high; if it is a greenish-blue colour it is well hung. There is really no need to hang wild duck, but a forkbender of a wild goose may hang for a week or two in an attempt to tenderise it.

Any badly shot game should be dealt with quickly as it will soon deteriorate.

Oven Ready

Have to hand a small sharp knife, a pair of stout kitchen scissors or secateurs and an old bucket for innards, head, feet etc.

Plucking

Pluck birds outdoors or in a shed over a box or dustbin lined with a large plastic bag. Start by fanning the wings and pulling out the primaries, then work in towards the body. To prevent the delicate breast skin from tearing, hold it taut as you remove the feathers, pulling them out in the direction of their growth a few at a time. Soft downy feathers may be removed by rubbing with the ball of the thumb. Work down to the legs and tail.

Skinning

If a bird has been damaged, it is much quicker to skin than pluck it. Cut off the head and clip off the wings and legs with secateurs. Lay the bird on its back, and with a sharp knife, cut the skin lightly along the breastbone and peel it off in one piece.

If only the breast meat is required, simply peel back the skin to expose the breast, then with a sharp knife, make a cut under the lower end of the breastbone, cut deeply along the ribs close to the wings and then using secateurs, cut through the collarbones. Remove the whole breast in one piece on the bone.

Drawing

Using a sharp knife, cut off the head at the top of the neck. Loosen the skin around the neck and draw out the windpipe and crop, taking care to avoid breaking the crop.

Cut off the neck close to the body, leaving the loose skin intact.

Make a cut above and below the vent and remove it. Gripping the bird around the breast with one hand, insert two fingers of the other hand into the body cavity. Reach up under the breastbone and pull out in one clean movement the heart, gizzard, liver, gall bladder and intestines. Keep the heart, gizzard and liver but discard both the gall bladder, without puncturing it, and the intestines.

Split the gizzard, peel off and discard the lining and contents and wash in cold water together with the heart, liver and neck which should be used for stock. The liver may be saved for pâté. Wipe the bird with a clean damp cloth, and finally cut off the feet.

A pheasant, unlike other game birds and wildfowl, has many strong tendons and sinews in its legs, though most of these can be removed: cut through the scaly skin right round the foot joint, then through the hard white tendon at the back of this joint. Break the joint and pull very hard. The foot should come away together with the tendons and sinews.

When preparing duck it is a good idea to remove the two small oil glands on the upper side of the parson's nose as they may give a musky flavour to the meat.

Woodcock and snipe should be plucked but not drawn except for the gizzard. Make a small cut above the thigh but below the breastbone, and with one finger locate and remove the gizzard. Skin the head and remove the eyes. Leave the feet on.

Keep dressed birds in the refrigerator, or store immediately in the freezer.

Freezing Game

Some people will never own a freezer because they prefer to eat only seasonal food. While I partly sympathise with this view, when faced with basketsful of runner beans from the garden or more pheasants than I can face in a week, freezing the surplus to eat later is the obvious and thrifty solution.

There is no virtue in freezing birds in their feathers unless you are really short of time and have a large number to handle. Feathered game takes up more room in the freezer, is awkward to handle and, once it has been thawed, plucked and drawn, it must be cooked and not refrozen raw, although it may be safely frozen after cooking.

Allow game to hang before freezing: this may be from three to ten days depending on the condition of the game, personal taste and weather conditions. On the other hand it is better to freeze wild duck as soon as possible, as hanging does not improve the flavour. In cold weather wild geese may hang for up to two weeks; this will help to tenderise older birds.

Before freezing, birds should be plucked or skinned and drawn. Snipe and woodcock should be plucked but not drawn with the exception of the gizzard which should be removed through a small incision in the side of the body. Wipe the birds inside and out and remove any visible shot, badly broken wings or legs.

Hares should be skinned, jointed or left whole, and soaked for twenty-four hours in cold salted water before freezing.

Wrap any sharp or protruding bones in foil and pack in heavy-gauge polythene. Expel all the air and seal the bag tightly. Whole breasts, drumsticks or individual hare joints may be frozen separately on a baking tray, then stored together in one large polythene bag so that you may choose the amount you need for a recipe. Finally, label the bag clearly, showing the species, whether young or old, and the date.

Game birds and hares will keep for up to a year, and wildfowl for six to nine months, though I have occasionally discovered game which has been stored for much longer than this and it has cooked perfectly.

When cooking a casserole or soup it is a good idea to make more than you need and freeze the surplus. This saves time and fuel and you will have a supply of instant meals.

Cooked game dishes must be thawed and thoroughly reheated.

Game pies may be frozen, but hot-water crust pastry tends to crumble once thawed.

Pâté may be frozen for two months, but it must be thawed slowly and completely before use.

Soup will keep for two months, but add eggs or cream when reheating.

Always use frozen birds in reverse order of storage, the earliest first, and plan to have plenty of room in the freezer at the start of each new season.

Grouse

Early on the 12 August, grouse are rushed from moor to breakfast table in an unseemly dash via pony express, helicopter, hot air balloon and taxi cab in a race that is fast becoming a rival to the Beaujolais Nouveau run. This truly wild game bird is in prime condition from the beginning of the season until mid-October.

Hang birds for one or two days in warm weather, up to a week in colder conditions. Young birds have soft feet, smooth legs, and the tip of the breastbone is soft. The lower mandible should break under the weight of the bird when held between thumb and first finger. Older birds have scaly legs with sharp or detached claws, and the tip of the breastbone is hard and sharp.

Young birds may be roasted whole or grilled if split in half and basted frequently. Cooking in an oven brick with wine and herbs is an alternative to roasting, especially if the birds are of doubtful age. Older birds should be used for casseroles, pies and pâtés.

Because of its diet of heather and berries, grouse has a unique flavour which is enhanced by the plainest cooking. Rowan, hawthorn or elderberry jelly are fine accompaniments.

Roast Grouse

Serves 4

4 young grouse
8 rashers streaky bacon
6 tbsp red wine
Salt and black pepper
Watercress and heather sprigs for garnish

Wrap two rashers of bacon round each bird so that the breast and legs are
covered.
Place in a roasting tin and cook in a hot oven 200C/400F/gas mark 6 for 45
minutes.
Place the birds onto a warm serving dish and keep hot.
Add the wine to the pan juices and season to taste to make a thin gravy.
Decorate the grouse with watercress and heather sprigs and serve with the
hot gravy, home-made fried breadcrumbs, and rowan or hawthorn jelly.

Grouse Véronique

Serves 4

Most kitchens today have a microwave as a compliment to a conventional oven. This recipe cooks equally well in either.
Instructions for a conventional oven are given in brackets.

2 young grouse	150ml/¼ pint single cream
100g/4oz mushrooms	½ tbsp cornflour
150ml/¼ pint chicken stock	100g/4oz seedless white grapes

Cut the grouse in halves using game shears or stout kitchen scissors.
Trim away the backbone and rib bones and remove any remaining innards.
Slice the mushrooms and place in a casserole.
Add the grouse halves.
Pour over the chicken stock, cover and cook on A5 or medium for 15 minutes (30 minutes in a moderate oven 180C/350F/gas mark 4).
Blend the cornflour with the cream and add to the casserole, together with the grapes.
Cook on high for 2 minutes (Return to the oven for a further 10 minutes).
Serve immediately with French beans and buttered noodles.

Tan Hill Grouse

Serves 3–4

This recipe is strictly for veterans with many moorland miles under their belts! Any strong local ale will do.

1 brace mature grouse	4 sticks celery, sliced (keep leaves for garnish)
100g/4oz bacon, chopped	300ml/½ pint Theakston's Old Peculiar
1 small onion, chopped	300ml/½ pint stock
2 carrots, diced	Bay leaf

Place the chopped vegetables, bacon and bay leaf in a flameproof casserole.
Add the grouse breast side down, and pour over the ale and stock.
Bring to the boil slowly, cover and simmer for 2 hours or until tender.
Remove the grouse and bacon from the casserole.
Pull off the legs and wings and cut away the breast meat.
Place the grouse and bacon on a warm serving dish, cover and keep hot.
Purée the softened vegetables in a blender or rub through a sieve.
Return the purée to the casserole and reheat gently.
Pour the sauce over the grouse and decorate with celery leaves.

Partridge

The partridge is claimed by many to be the 'king of game birds'. It has a mild and delicate flavour, especially the English or grey partridge which is often preferred at table to the more common French or red-legged partridge.

During a mild autumn hang partridge for only three to four days; this may be increased to up to a week in colder weather. Young grey partridge have dark beaks and olive-coloured legs, old birds have grey beaks and silver legs. The two outer primary feathers on young French partridge have cream-coloured tips, and in young English and French birds these feathers will have pointed tips easily distinguished from the more rounded feathers of older birds.

Young birds may be plainly roasted or grilled, or cooked in a mild flavoured wine or cream sauce. Older birds should be used in casseroles or game pies.

Partridge Provençal
Serves 4

The warm Mediterranean climate of Provence produces large sweet tomatoes, olives, garlic and aromatic herbs.

2 plump young French partridge	*For the marinade:*
1 tbsp olive oil	2 tbsp olive oil
4 cloves garlic	2 tbsp red wine vinegar
6 large tomatoes	1 tbsp chopped parsley
2 tsps tomato purée	½ tbsp chopped thyme
100g/4oz black olives, stoned	½ tbsp chopped oregano
Fresh parsley and oregano for garnish	Salt and pepper

Split the partridges into halves, remove any remaining innards and place in a shallow dish.
Mix together the ingredients for the marinade and spoon it over the meat.
Leave in a cool place for 24 hours, basting frequently.
Drain the meat and reserve the marinade.
Heat 1 tbsp oil in a large frying pan, add the whole garlic cloves and partridge halves and cook slowly for 10 minutes on each side.
Scald the tomatoes in boiling water for 15 seconds. Pour off the water and replace it with cold. The skin then comes off easily.
Chop the tomatoes finely.
Remove the garlic, add the reserved marinade, chopped tomatoes and tomato purée, cover and cook gently for 20 minutes.
Place the birds on a serving dish and keep hot.
Add the olives to the sauce and heat through gently.

Pour the sauce over the birds, garnish with herbs and serve with rice tossed with a pinch of saffron and small pieces of crisply fried bacon.

Lord's Ground Partridge

Serves 4

This recipe captures the flavours of autumn in the English countryside.

4 English partridge	150ml/5fl oz single cream
450g/1lb Cox apples	Salt and pepper
300ml/½ pint white wine	Chopped parsley for garnish
150ml/¼ pint stock	

Cut the partridge in half using game shears or kitchen scissors, trim away the backbone and small rib bones.

Place the birds in a flameproof casserole and add the apples, wine, stock and seasoning. Bring to the boil and simmer gently for 1–1½ hours.

Remove the birds and keep them hot on a serving dish.

Rub the apples through a sieve and return the purée to the casserole.

Add the cream and heat through gently.

Spoon the sauce over the partridge and sprinkle with chopped parsley.

Pheasant

The cock pheasant with his flamboyant colouring, and the more soberly dressed hen, must be the best known of the British game birds. Though less favoured for its culinary merits than the more subtle-tasting partridge, it is undoubtedly the most versatile bird in the kitchen. Its gamey flavour marries well with a variety of fruits, vegetables, herbs and spices and lends itself to European and Asian cuisine. It is suitable for celebrations that call for the family silver, or as a more humble shoot supper, or as beaters' fare.

A young bird shot in October may only need to hang for three days, but for an old forkbender shot in January, two weeks would not be too long. A young cock pheasant has rounded spurs which become sharper with age. A young hen has soft feet which later become rough and hard.

Traditional roast pheasant is served with bacon, fried breadcrumbs or game chips and garnished colourfully with cranberries, watercress and the cock's magnificent tail feathers!

Festive Pheasant

Serves 4

A more unusual way to serve pheasant either hot or cold for a special occasion. A small game bird is boned and filled with a mushroom and bacon stuffing and sewn inside a boned pheasant. When carved, each slice contains a layer of meat from both birds with the stuffing in the centre.

1 young pheasant, boned	100g/4oz breadcrumbs
1 young partridge or grouse, boned	25g/1oz butter
4 rashers streaky bacon	1 egg, beaten
100g/4oz lean bacon, chopped	½ tsp ground mace
100g/4oz mushrooms, chopped	Black pepper

Lightly fry the chopped bacon and mushrooms in the butter.
Mix these with the breadcrumbs and bind together with the beaten egg. Season with the mace and black pepper.
Open the boned pheasant and lay it skin-side down. Open the boned partridge or grouse and place it on top of the pheasant. Spread the stuffing over the meat.
Pull the edges of the pheasant together and sew up with fine string, making sure there are no gaps. Reshape the joint to resemble a pheasant and cover with the streaky bacon rashers.

Place in a roasting tin and cook in a moderate oven 180C/350F/gas mark 4 for 1½ hours.

Place the meat on a warm serving dish and use the pan juices to make a thin gravy. Before serving, surround the meat with seasonal vegetables of mixed colours.

To serve cold, place the meat on a bed of radicchio lettuce, garnish with watercress and carve the first few slices to reveal the different layers. Serve with a selection of salads.

Maharajah's Pheasant

Serves 4

The top ten list of the best ever Shots in the world must surely include the Maharajah Dhuleep Singh of Lahore, known locally in East Anglia as the Black Prince. This easy recipe with an Indian flavour uses the breast meat from two pheasants. Use the legs for a casserole, pâté, or soup.

> 2 whole pheasant breasts, skinned
> 1 tbsp Tandoori Mix Spice Marinade
> 3 tbsp natural yoghurt
> 1 tbsp lemon juice
> 1 tbsp vinegar
> Lemon wedges

With a sharp knife, carefully remove the meat from the breastbone and make two or three diagonal slits in each breast.

Place the meat in a shallow dish.

Blend the spice mix, yoghurt, lemon juice and vinegar into a smooth paste and use it to coat the meat, rubbing it in with the back of a spoon.

Cover and leave overnight in the refrigerator.

Place the pheasant breasts on a greased baking tray and bake at 180C/350F/gas mark 4 for 15 minutes. Baste with the remaining marinade and cook for a further 15 minutes.

Transfer to a hot dish, garnish with the lemon wedges and serve immediately with pilau rice and a green salad.

Snipe and Woodcock

Snipe and woodcock are testing targets for even the most accomplished shot. A right and left at woodcock, the equivalent of a golfer's 'hole in one', opens the door to membership of the exclusive Shooting Times Woodcock Club.

Although snipe are in season from 12 August they are not in prime condition until October or November. As with all game, how long you hang is according to personal taste and depending on the weather; this may be for two to four days, although some people choose not to hang them at all.

Traditionally, snipe and woodcock are not drawn before cooking, with the exception of the gizzard. The head should be skinned and the eyes removed, and head and neck are then brought round to the side of the body and passed through the legs and body to act as a skewer.

As snipe and woodcock are unlikely to feature regularly in the bag, they should be treated with reverence and simplicity.

Snipe on Toast
Serves 2

A couple of snipe on toast washed down with a glass of champagne is said to have been Winston Churchill's favourite breakfast. Make sure that the champagne is in the refrigerator overnight!

A couple of snipe	Melted butter
2 rashers bacon	Pepper
2 slices bread	Watercress for garnish

Toast the bread on one side only.

Place the snipe on the untoasted side of the bread and put them in the bottom of a grill pan. Place a rasher of bacon over each bird. Cook under a hot grill for 10 minutes or until the bacon is brown. Remove the bacon, baste with the melted butter and add a shake of pepper. Reduce the heat and continue to cook for a further 5 minutes.

Place each snipe on toast onto a hot plate, spoon the pan juices over the birds and serve with the bacon and a sprig of watercress.

Woodcock au Naturel

The trail of the woodcock melts and mingles with the cooking juices to produce a natural sauce which is the crowning glory of this highly prized game bird.

A couple of woodcock	Oil for frying
25g/1oz softened butter	Salt and pepper
4 rashers streaky bacon	Lemon wedges for garnish
2 thick slices bread	

Cover the birds with softened butter. Wrap two rashers of bacon round the breast and thighs of each bird.

Place them in a small roasting tin, cover with foil and cook in a hot oven 200C/400F/gas mark 6 for 45 minutes.

Remove the foil, baste the birds with the cooking juices and cook for a further 15 minutes uncovered.

Fry the bread in the oil until crisp and golden.

Place the woodcock on the fried bread, lightly season the pan juices and pour the sauce over the birds. Decorate with lemon wedges and serve at once.

Wild Duck and Goose

Duck

There are several species of wild duck, but the mallard and the smaller wigeon are most frequently eaten. The smallest and often the most highly regarded for its subtle flavour is the teal. Duck do not need hanging as the fatty flesh tends to deteriorate rather than improve.

Whole birds are best plainly roasted, though the body cavity may be filled with herbs, onions or oranges. Honey or Seville marmalade brushed on the skin adds a crisp, sweet glaze. A stuffing of sage and onion, or apricot and walnuts may be served with the duck as well as the traditional apple or orange sauce.

Geese

By far the largest wild goose which may be shot in Britain is that native of North America, the Canada goose, introduced here as an ornamental bird to enhance the lakes of country estates. The Canada provides good sport and is usually considered to be the best flavoured of all the geese.

As a general rule, in cold weather geese may hang for up to two weeks to help to tenderise the meat.

191

Wild geese are difficult to age accurately. Young birds have a flexible underbill and brightly coloured legs, and they lack the strong, clear-cut markings of the adult bird. Early in the season young geese have a V-shaped notch in the tail feather. If in doubt, treat the bird as old!

Young birds may be roasted with a herb or fruit stuffing and served with a fruit jelly or sauce. The addition of wine, cider, fruit juice or stock will help to keep the birds moist. Older birds need long, gentle cooking and also make excellent pâté.

Honey-glazed Mallard
Serves 4

Young September mallard fattened on grain from the stubble fields usually have plenty of natural fat and should be cooked on a trivet so that any excess fat may be poured off.

> Brace of mallard
> 2 tbsp clear honey
> Watercress or sprigs of fresh sage for garnish

Place the mallard breast-side down on a trivet in a roasting tin. Using a pastry brush, spread half of the honey over the backs of the birds.
Roast in a moderately hot oven 200C/400F/Gas Mark 6 for 45 minutes. Turn the birds over and brush the remaining honey over the legs and breasts. Cook breast-side up for a further 45 minutes. The skin should be crisp and brown.
Place the birds on a serving dish and keep hot. Skim off any excess fat from the roasting tin and make a thin gravy.
Garnish the mallard with watercress or sage sprigs and serve with an apple or orange sauce and fresh vegetables.

Spiced Canada Goose
Serves 4–6

Wild goose is best roasted with stock, wine or cider as this helps to keep the flesh moist.

> 1 young Canada goose, oven-ready
> 1 apple and 1 orange
> 12 cloves
> 300ml/½ pint dry cider
> 2 tbsp soft brown sugar
> 1 tsp cinnamon
> 1 tsp dry mustard
> 2 tbsp wine vinegar
> Watercress for garnish

Mix the sugar, cinnamon and mustard with the wine vinegar.

Spike the apple and orange with the cloves and place inside the body cavity.

Truss the goose and place breast-side down in a roasting tin. Pour over the cider. Cover with foil and cook in a fairly hot oven 200C/400F/Gas Mark 6 for 1 hour.

Turn the goose over and brush the spiced mixture over the breast and legs. Cover and cook for a further 1 hour.

Remove the foil and cook for another 20 minutes or until the skin of the goose is crisp. Transfer the goose to a serving dish and keep hot.

Use the pan juices to make a thin gravy. Decorate the goose with watercress and serve with Brussels sprouts and chestnuts.

Hare

For centuries it was believed that hares had mystical and supernatural powers. To the ancient Britons they were sacred; in the Middle Ages their association with witchcraft led to the belief that the only way to kill a witch-hare was with a silver bullet! Evidence that the hare was hunted for meat from very early times can be seen in Roman, Greek and Egyptian art.

The cost of preparing a hare so that it was palatable was far beyond the means of ordinary country folk, so a poached hare would be sold to the gentry and was worth more than a week's pay. Game records from large estates in the early nineteenth century show that only young hares went to the table and that they were usually soaked in a quart of milk to make the meat paler and less strongly flavoured, and then cooked in ale or rough cider and basted with a pint of cream!

A young hare or leveret has soft ears, a smooth coat and small white teeth; the coat of an adult hare becomes wavy and grey, the ears are hard and dry and the teeth grow long and yellow. In cold weather hares should hang head down and unpaunched for seven to ten days.

After skinning and paunching, the blood that has collected in the rib-cage may be saved and used to enrich the sauce of a classic jugged hare. Wash the meat thoroughly in cold water and leave to soak in cold salted water for twenty-four hours; rinse again before cooking or freezing.

Only young hares should be roasted; a forcemeat and herb stuffing and plenty of fat bacon laid on the hare will help to prevent the fat-free meat from becoming dry. Older hares may be marinated in cider, beer or wine and should then receive long, slow cooking. The flavour is improved by cooking one day and reheating the next.

Green Ginger Hare

Serves 4

1 saddle of hare in two pieces	*For the marinade:*
2 front legs	3 tbsp green ginger wine
2.5cm/1in piece root ginger	2 tbsp olive oil
	1 small onion, chopped
8 rashers streaky bacon	8 black peppercorns, crushed
4 tbsp single cream	

Place the hare joints in a flameproof casserole.

Mix together the ingredients for the marinade, spoon over the hare and leave in the refrigerator for at least 24 hours, turning the joints occasionally. Remove the hare joints but leave the marinade in the casserole. Peel the root ginger and grate it over the hare, then wrap two rashers of bacon round each joint.

Return the meat to the casserole, cover with a lid or tinfoil and bake in a moderate oven 160C/325F/gas mark 3 for two hours.

Remove the hare and keep hot on a serving dish. Add the cream to the casserole and heat through gently.

Pour the sauce over the hare and serve with potatoes tossed in parsley and a green vegetable.

Potted Hare

Serves 8

An ideal recipe for an older hare, in which the cooked meat is blended to make a smooth-textured pâté. Serve with French bread for picnics or light lunches, or with Melba toast as a first course.

1 hare, jointed	Ground nutmeg
1 onion, sliced	100g/4oz butter, melted
2 bay leaves	1 tbsp sherry
Salt and 6 peppercorns	Black pepper
Grated rind and juice of 1 lemon	Fresh herbs for garnish

Place the hare in a large saucepan with the sliced onion, bay leaves, salt and peppercorns. Cover with water, bring to the boil and simmer gently for three hours or until the meat is tender. Leave to cool.

Remove the meat from the bones and place in a food processor. Add the melted butter, sherry, grated rind and juice of the lemon, salt, black pepper and nutmeg and blend until smooth. If necessary add some of the hare stock to make a firm mixture.

Spoon the pâté into small pots and chill thoroughly. Decorate with fresh herbs before serving.

14
Various Essentials

Insurance

The shooting field is a dangerous place and no-one in his right mind should venture into it without insurance. Accidents can happen in the best regulated organisations, and you only need but one in a lifetime to cause disaster. To have oneself insured against death or injury is prudent, but it is equally important to be insured against accident caused by you to a third party.

The risk in the shooting field is that of the dangerous shot, the once-in-a-lifetime moment of mad carelessness, the stumble, the dropped gun, the deceitful woodcock, and few are those who can claim never to have erred. Sometimes trespassers stray to places they should not, and the most obscure bush might conceal a picnicker, bird-watcher or courting couple.

My shoot is typical of many in that it insists on every Gun being fully covered, and that includes guests, beaters on beaters' days, stray visitors, and anyone else in a position to do damage. Membership of at least two of the national shooting bodies includes good third party cover in the subscription, and one can do a good deal worse than plump for that. I would not be happy to shoot in the company of anyone not fully covered.

The farm or estate will be insured against any accident involving the farm equipment, gates, trailers and tractors used to tow shoot personnel round on a shooting day. This is vital and it is important that the shoot captain confirms that insurance is up to date before the start of each season. Those who drive farm machinery should be qualified to do so. The Health and Safety at Work Act makes it a crime to behave in a dangerous way in the place of work, and it is not good enough to allow a lad whose only experience of tractor driving is a week's corn carting in the summer to be responsible for driving twenty human beings on muddy droves.

My shoot learned this lesson the hard way. An inexperienced driver managed to overturn a waggonload of beaters in a field gateway. It was a mercy that nobody was seriously injured, as the situation was potentially lethal. The one minor back sprain was more than enough, and I dread to think what lawsuits would have accrued had things been worse.

There are rules relating to the type of vehicle you may use to transport personnel round farms. If it is not roofed, the sides must be well above the waist of a sitting man; seats must be fixed, and if straw bales, then they must be tied securely; steps in and out must be safe and firm; a trailer of over a certain weight must be fitted with brakes: a wise shoot organiser will check the legislation carefully. Everyone is very friendly and pleasant until an accident—and then you discover who your friends really are, and how folk you thought you knew well can change for the worse the moment they sniff a profitable court case. A cynical view, you might say, but sadly its truth is proved all too often. Each season shoot trailers should be carefully serviced after the summer layoff; nor is it difficult to provide a cover or tilt to keep the passengers dry and out of the wind and flying mud from tractor wheels while en route. A brief respite in comparative comfort between drives makes all the difference to *their* enjoyment.

Transport and the Game Cart

Some shoots have made quite a feature of their transport and have equipped themselves with converted buses, reconditioned tradesman's vans fitted with seats and gunracks, up to the lucky one or two which really do things in style and have preserved one of the original horse-drawn shooting brakes.

Traditionally an aged shoot servant is given responsibility for the game cart, someone who is a little too frail to beat any longer but who remains keen and interested. His duty is an important one. Respect for the quarry alive and dead is a mark of the sportsman, and a dead game bird must not be thrown anyhow into the well of a Landrover or among the muddy feet of a dozen dogs. It should be hung carefully by the neck as soon as possible after being shot, either singly or braced in a place where the air can circulate and where it will stiffen naturally. There are various systems for doing this, from poles across the back of open trucks, to special racks with hooks bolted into the back of pick-ups.

The game cart man will sort out any damaged birds and put them on one side in case they end up by mistake in someone's brace when the shoot is over. At various times during the day he will transfer the bag to the game larder; this varies from shoot to shoot, but in each case the game can be hung up neatly, again with air round it, out of the reach of dogs and in a way which shows it off nicely. A good row of well displayed game is a treat for the eye at the end of the day. Some great estates have purpose-built game larders of great antiquity and beauty with game hooks innumerable and underfloor water-cooling systems. Most of us today have to make do with a cart shed.

At the end, the keeper will ask for so many brace to be selected for the Guns, and these birds should be undamaged, clean and young so that they are fitting for the table of a guest. The remainder of the bag is distributed to various friends, some for the house and some for the game dealer. He, too, appreciates shot birds which have been looked after carefully. Our game cart man was Eric Playle from Essex and a better man at the job it would be hard to find.

The Associations

It is right and proper that the shooting man should support, through personal membership, at least one of his national organisations. Some say it

is a pity that there are more than one, and that a single voice to represent us all—anglers, hound hunters and shooting folk—would be better than a fragmented defence; but such a debate is for another arena, and not here. All field sports have come under great pressure and received a great deal of largely ill-informed criticism from an unsympathetic and mainly urban public, many of whom would lose no sleep at all if country sports were to go.

There is also the matter of research and development, of maintaining a staff of experts to help with members' enquiries, and the insurance cover already mentioned. Keeping a close watch on the ever-changing political scene is also important nowadays.

The game shooter is served principally by three organisations and it is proper that he should join at least one of them.

The British Association for Shooting and Conservation (BASC)

Founded originally for wildfowlers and called the Wildfowlers Association of Great Britain and Ireland (WAGBI), the BASC is the body for the all-round shooting man and woman. Based at Marford Mill in Rossett it has a large staff which keeps a watching brief on the political scene both at home and in the EC. The BASC publishes a quarterly journal; it runs a conservation and research programme; organises funding for the purchase of, for example, wetlands under threat; supports a large network of local clubs nationwide; and generates good grassroots support. It has taken positive steps to raise the quality of the new entrant to the sport with its Proficiency Award Scheme which puts entrants through a series of lectures and practical tests to prepare them for a sport which is a minefield of do's and don'ts. Some affiliated clubs insist on all new members having gained this award.

The BASC runs a popular and successful Gamekeeper's Fair, also local roadshows and safaris, and it maintains a high profile at national events such as the CLA Game Fair. A strong regional network ensures that the common touch is maintained, and that recruitment is generally good. The subscription includes the all-important insurance which I have urged all shooting folk to take out as standard: joining the BASC is as good a way as any of ensuring vital cover as well as the other advantages.

The Game Conservancy

This organisation is of special interest to the game shooter, and its headquarters are at Fordingbridge in Hampshire. It is a registered charity and so is prevented from entering the political arena in any save a detached manner. Its brief has been to study in depth our native game birds and their habitats, other creatures within their orbit (song birds on feed rides or butterflies in game coverts, for example), and thus inevitably the whole broad sweep of conservation of the British countryside: game and game habitats may not be studied in a vacuum.

A staff of international experts has carried out a great deal of learned research which is highly regarded worldwide. Projects range from the highly practical (how to build an effective release pen), to the fairly esoteric, such as the effect of fish populations on insect stocks and hence on the survival rate of mallard ducklings. The problem seems to be fairly identified as the conflict between agricultural interests and healthy game bird habitats, and we do well to remember that a place which is good for game is good for many other things too.

The rapacious farming of the sixties and seventies gave us a countryside bereft of wild flowers ('weeds'), insects ('pests'), birds ('destroyers of crops') and hedgerows, ('valuable space which ought to be used to grow more barley—that nobody will ever eat'). Wild game birds diminished in the wild to an alarming degree, notably the grey partridge which the Game

Conservancy took for its emblem. Thanks largely to the GC's efforts, many species are increasing, and the quality of the countryside has improved. The grey partridge remains in dire straits.

The GC offers professional guidance to members needing advice on how to improve their shoots, the scheme being run by a team of regional advisers. Practical tips and down-to-earth management strategies, from making feeders on the cheap to controlling vermin, are there for the asking, whether your ground is a mere handful of acres or a great estate of many thousands. Their publications on various aspects of shoot management are essential reading for anyone who takes shooting and conservation seriously.

The British Fieldsports Society (BFSS)

The BFSS has an all-round brief for all country sports, and while political difficulties have caused it to focus closely on the hound sports, it has a high profile and proven track record in shooting and fishing. Falconry, coursing—you name it and the BFSS has a brief for it. There is no doubt that in the past this was the body exclusively for hunting folk, but steps have been taken to widen the brief. A good example is the production in 1989 of a magnificent video, 'The Shooting Year' ('A Three-Legged Stool') which is devoted entirely to game shooting and enlightened keepering practices.

A particular strength of the BFSS is its political clout, and the fact that its base is in London offices, the only major fieldsports organisation to be so well and prudently appointed. Handy for Parliament, it is well placed for quick lobbying in the case of legislation which affects fieldsports; it is swift to react to troubles which threaten us, and has a PR department second to none. It is unusual to be unable to get a message through, even at weekends and holidays, and in my view the modern BFSS has shed its ancient hang-ups and operates a tight ship.

There is a network of regional chairmen and their staffs and many volunteers who maintain a high profile at fieldsports' fairs and other events. Bucket collections are organised at country shows and point-to-points, and revenue from a sales department and special events help the funds; the subscription includes third party insurance against accidents in the sporting field.

Support for our national bodies is important for more than just the practical benefits. In this day and age it is not good enough for any shooter to go out and enjoy his sport with a clear conscience, knowing that others who *are* members are helping to protect and advance its interests, whilst he is an outsider.

Magazines and Books

He who commits himself to the shooting field must do so with 100 per cent enthusiasm. I do not believe game shooting is, or should be, a sport into which one can dip at random, or approach in a casual way. It is too important for that. Those who are keen eat, drink and think shooting at all times; when they are asleep they dream about it. Knowledge of the history and practice of the sport is important to savour the finer details.

He who emerges from the shooting waggon—stands, shoots, returns to the waggon and so home—misses a great deal. What went into putting those birds over him? What are the tactics of running a shooting day? How educated is his eye to the finer points, the play of the sunlight on the berries in the hedge over which he expects the partridges to erupt at any minute? Does he know his birds and beasts, appreciate enough of what is going on to involve himself in the sport of his companions? He may have no dog, but what does he know of their training and the way they are deployed?

One way of sharing this in-depth involvement is to meet and mix with other shooting people—in fact they tend to find each other out in any community, and just talking, sharing experiences and listening is useful. A modest library of shooting books is rewarding. There are many on the market, from times past and of today—and collecting shooting books can become addictive: there are those who fill their shelves with treasured volumes, for many of the old Victorian works have become collectable and expensive. The roots of what we do today were seeds then, and while many of the details and legislation may have changed, the basics remain much the same.

Who could not thrill to accounts of big bags on the great estates in the golden age? Lord Walsingham, the finest Shot in Britain and his record bag of grouse shot in Yorkshire; the archaic, how-to-do-it books about gamekeeping; adventures by the covertside and on the moor; successes and disappointments; the great wildfowlers of yesteryear who went afloat in their punts with those huge guns and came home loaded to the gunnels with wigeon and brent geese: such yarns are the fabric of the sport we enjoy today, and knowing about the history places the present in perspective and makes the reader a fuller shooting man.

The shrewd collector will discover that the stories of shooting days have a longer shelf life than the how-to-do-it books, for the practical aspect is very much standard and well documented. What cannot be reiterated are the adventures of the great days and of noted sportsmen long dead.

Further reading, but of a more ephemeral type, can be had in the form of the magazines and periodicals about our sport. The most famous and the longest-running is *The Shooting Times*, which seeks weekly to entertain and inform with news, letters from readers, and articles. In a rapidly changing political climate it is wise for the shooting man to be well-informed, and especially in the dull, out-of-season months, it is good to be reminded of happy days past and those still to come when he opens the envelope each week. There are other magazines too, some of them monthly, and the journals published by the national associations are well worth reading.

A fine picture is as good a way as any to be reminded of memorable places and sporting occasions: a superb John Paley painting of partridges topping the quickthorn hedge on a September day will revive an old memory as you sit in your armchair. There are many excellent sporting artists producing wonderful work: John Paley, Rodger McPhail, Will Garfit, Julian Novorol,

Derick Brown and Jonathan Yule are among my favourites, and I can look at their work for hours. Care must be taken with selection, as any picture must be one with which you are happy to live for many years, and so frequently a canvas has one tiny, annoying detail—the wing of one bird might not be quite to your fancy, or the shooter is aiming at what you feel to be the wrong bird. Take a long time before you make up your mind, and be prepared to wait if things are not perfectly to your liking.

A camera is a useful companion, for photographs of those special places and people will capture the essence of a happy day for ever—a picture is, as Confucius observed, worth a thousand words. Modern cameras are small and neat enough to be slipped into a coat pocket at no inconvenience. It is important to record *at the time* the names and the date if you are not to end up with a pile of photographs, half of the value of which is lost because you cannot remember exactly who is in them, or where and when it was taken.

The Game Book

I believe in the importance of keeping a shooting diary. Great pleasure may be had from re-reading past adventures, and recalling places and names where you have enjoyed interesting sport. Some game diaries are of the old estate record variety where there is room to record only the details of game shot with a parsimonious space for 'Comments'. The comments are the best part, for fifty pheasants here reads much the same as fifty pheasants there. The interesting things are the little adventures, the sudden change in the weather, a brilliant shot at a high bird, an unexpected woodcock, a narrow shave, a fine retrieve by a young dog, what happened at lunch—those are the things which make a shooting day memorable, irrespective of the size of the bag. There should be room in the game book to glue photographs, maps and game cards, and the pin feathers of snipe and woodcock, so that the record is as complete, accurate and above all, personal as you can make it.

If you cannot buy such a book, then make up your own from an old ledger with space for inscribing the date and place, those present, and the bag; and then a large area on the opposite page which may be as long or as short as you wish, for your own comments on the day. Make filling in the book a matter of routine like cleaning the gun or seeing to the dog; the endless pleasure of your outings, recollected in the tranquillity of your armchair, will become the promise of the future.

The Local Club

As well as joining your national association, you might find it of benefit to join the local fields sports club. Most districts have one (a full list is available from the BASC), and it will serve as a good way of keeping in touch with what is going on, with other local sportsmen, and maybe learning something new. Such clubs tend to meet monthly and organise a variety of events including clay shooting, conservation courses, lectures and practical demonstrations, such as gundog training, as well as events concerning other, non-shooting sports—it does no harm to be reminded that all field sports are bedfellows, and that it is in our mutual interest to stick together. The shooting man ought to know about hunting and fishing, even if he will never actively participate in them.

These are troubled times for all country sports and while it may be tempting to denigrate another man's sport in order to show your own in a better light, at the end of the day we stand and fall together; so when the call comes to lobby your MP about, say, a hunting issue, then rise to the occasion and do your bit, even if you have no intention of ever sitting astride a horse. For the rest, the video evenings, the acquisition of club rough shooting, wildfowling or maybe driven shooting, learning from experts about dogs, gear and tactics—all this can add to your expertise and your enjoyment.

The Vehicle

It is quite likely that you will have the use of the family saloon—and if you are lucky it is an estate—for your shooting days. Although two car families are quite frequent in this affluent age, if you have just the one set of wheels it is good policy not to bring it home caked in mud, dog hairs, blood and feathers. The memsahib does not care for such souvenirs, which have a magical knack of spreading themselves thinly on any surface within twenty paces.

Remember the Wellie bag to store muddy boots: it is a good investment. Most shooting families, especially those with dogs, have an estate car or at least a hatchback, and for these a heavy-duty boot-lining is useful: there is the 'Armadillo', and others on the market now, too. Purpose-made for each make of car and constructed of tough fibre-glass, the Armadillo fits neatly in the back, and into it you may leave anything which is likely to make a mess. When you get home you simply lift the whole thing out and leave it in the shed, and if it is filthy you just run the hosepipe over it to wash it down; the interior of the car, however, is as clean as when you set off. You may carry bricks, cement and sand loose in this device.

For dogs obtain one of the travelling dog boxes, usually made of aluminium with a cage front. These may be had to fit different makes of vehicle. A dog left in the back of a car for long periods while his master roisters in front of the fire with fellow Guns after a good day out is a prey to many temptations, especially if he has been neither fed nor dried. I have seen the best dogs in the world eat dead game and chew up equipment left with them, simply as a way of getting something in their stomachs after an exhausting day working. The dog box of the Lintran or Portapet type will prevent all this, providing the dog with a safe and secure place in which it can curl up, and giving its master peace of mind in the knowledge that his £100 boots are safe from punctures.

The back of the vehicle should be well organised, with equipment laid out and packed logically and not thrown into a pile. On arrival at the shoot it is good to be able to assemble your kit methodically, without rush or panic, giving an easy start to the day.

The lucky shooting man is the one who has an extra vehicle which he can devote at least in part to his sport. This might be one of the many 4WD all-terrain vehicles or a van in which he can keep some of his equipment, sparing the family car from rough service and leaving it available for other members of the family on shooting days.

I have used a Subaru pickup truck with a fibre-glass back for some years and found it very useful. The four-wheel-drive is handy for driving in muddy places, and I can get all my equipment in the back besides a dog box. Some shooters fit a special secure unit inside the back, which is to be recommended in many ways, as a gun left in a car is very much at risk. Any car thief worth his name can open most cars in seconds, and the thought of your valuable gun left in it, unsecured and therefore at risk for a couple of hours at the end of a shooting day, is worrying. Certainly the weapon should be out of sight, maybe hidden beneath the seats; and in truth the security box does make sense, although it is an expensive item. Other useful things should also be kept in the vehicle, such as a boot jack for pulling off muddy boots, a torch, jump leads and spare cartridges.

As a final word, always remember that if you are going to a strange shoot, plan your route with care and allow plenty of time for the journey. As we have observed, so many shoots are hidden down obscure tracks and country lanes: quarter of an hour late, and you never seem to recover from the fluster of setting up; arrive ten minutes early, and your whole day is improved.

Index

Numbers in *italic* indicate illustrations